THE STORY OF
SUTTON
COLDFIELD

ROGER LEA

First published in 2003 by Sutton Publishing Limited

Reprinted in 2011 by
The History Press,
The Mill, Brimscombe Port,
Stroud, Gloucestershire, GL5 2QG
www.thehistorypress.co.uk

British Library Cataloguing in Publication Data
A catalogue record for this book is available from the British Library

ISBN 978 0 7509 2843 4

All pictures and maps are from the author's collection unless specified otherwise.

Typeset in 10½/16½pt Galliard.
Typesetting and origination by
Sutton Publishing Limited.
Printed and bound in England

Contents

ONE

Beginnings

Sutton Coldfield, on the north side of the city of Birmingham, is an historic town. It is first recorded in 1086 but was already in existence before that, and the discovery and study of archaeological remains and features has thrown light on much earlier periods. Prehistoric people came to what is now Sutton Coldfield, and made use of the natural resources which they found here. Our history therefore begins with a review of the natural resources of the prehistoric landscape, many of which were determined by the geology of the area.

Geological time deals in millions and tens of millions of years, during which continents formed and reformed and shifted their relative positions around the globe. Vast deposits of sediment accumulated on the sea bed and low-lying land, only to be raised up and buckled by the processes of mountain-building, and then thrust below sea-level again in another era. After 4,000 million years of these immense processes the geological record of a place can be studied by seeing what rocks lie below the surface, using the simple principle that the deeper rocks are older than the ones above them.

Sutton Coldfield is situated on rock deposited in the Triassic Period, which lasted from 245 million to 208 million years ago. At that time the Midlands of England formed a low-lying part of the world continent known as Pangaea, and were at the same latitude as the Sahara Desert is now. There were high mountain ranges to the south, and deposits of sand and pebbles were formed in the low-lying desert by the seasonal rivers and occasional floods rushing down from these mountains. Later in the period the climate became less arid and a rise of sea-level meant that the deposits were often formed under water, giving rise to a mixture of sandstones and marls.

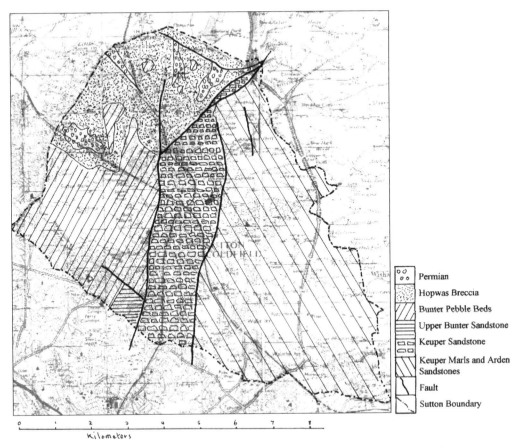

The solid geology of Sutton Coldfield. Redrawn from the Geological Survey of England and Wales (1924).

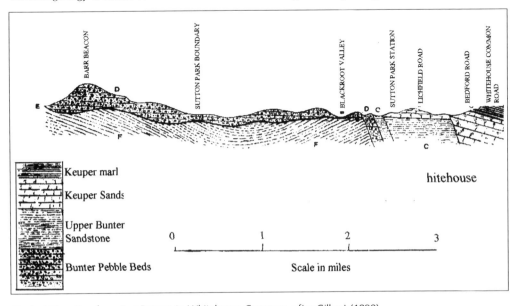

Geological section from Barr Beacon to Whitehouse Common, after Gilbert (1890).

In England the Triassic rocks occur in a band from Exeter to Teesside, and through Cheshire up to Preston – to the north and west they have mostly been eroded away leaving older formations at the surface, while to the south and east they are overlaid by vast deposits of more recent strata. Triassic rocks have been studied in various parts of the world, and a sequence within the Triassic Period has been noted. The geological map of Sutton shows part of the sequence, with the earliest deposits to the west.

The Bunter Pebble Beds which underlie Barr Beacon and Sutton Park have proved inhospitable to cultivation. For a long time they were good for nothing but heathland, and this area was branded the 'Coldfield' because it was so barren. To the east, these beds were thrust down at a fault-line and succeeded by a later formation, the Lower Keuper Sandstone. This rather crumbly sandstone gives rise to fertile soils, but cannot be used for building as it is so friable. It forms an excellent aquifer, supplying abundant drinking water from shallow wells – many of the finest beers of the Midlands are based on water from this formation.

An outcrop of Keuper Sandstone in Somerville Road, near Wyndley Lane.

A little further east is another fault-line, thrusting the Lower Keuper Sandstone down to be succeeded by the Upper Keuper Sandstone and Keuper marls. This pattern of parallel faults bounding the Lower Keuper Sandstone extends from the north of Sutton through Birmingham to Bromsgrove, and it was along this sandstone ridge that a number of settlements were established. The beds to the east, now usually known as the Arden sandstones and marls, are much more variable; bands of sandstone occur, which, like the Upper Keuper Sandstone at the base, can be quarried for building, while the marly deposits were useful for brickmaking. The fertility of the soils formed on these beds is variable.

The geological map shows that this description is a simplification of a very complicated arrangement. The underlying Permian strata is occasionally exposed,

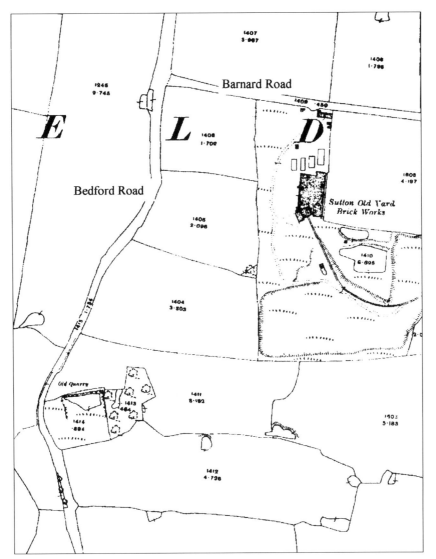

Part of the 1913 edition Ordnance Survey 25-inch map near Good Hope Hospital, showing a stone quarry and a brickworks; the fault-line separating the sandstone beds from the marl deposits used for brickmaking runs north–south between them.

while in the north of Sutton are outcrops of a particularly stony deposit, intermediate between Permian and Triassic, known as the Hopwas Breccia. To the south are the Bunter Sands, which spread across Kingstanding to Hockley and were extensively quarried for industrial use. The Permian strata are known as the Hamstead beds; beneath the Permian lies the Carboniferous or coal measures, and there was a coal mine at Hamstead. A trial shaft was sunk near Walmley in October 1873 in the hope of finding workable coal seams at depth, but without success.

The map only shows the solid geology, the basic beds being covered in many areas by up to 30 feet of drift. The drift dates from a much later geological period, when the general topography, that is, the hills and valleys we see today, had been formed, and England was in its present position on the globe. The ice ages of the Pleistocene Period, beginning about 2 million years ago, spread ice sheets and glaciers across most of northern Europe, retreating in warmer spells and advancing again as the climate changed. A stone-age handaxe recently found in Sutton proves that animals such as elk, wild horses and mammoths were being hunted here by Neanderthal Man in one of these warmer spells over 50,000 years ago. The most extensive glaciation extended as far south as the Thames Valley, and as the ice sheet slowly melted its burden of stones, soil and clay, which had mingled with the ice in its grinding advance, was deposited on the surface. These glacial deposits, often known as boulder clay, are very variable and often poorly drained, but they contain some flint, which was much used in prehistoric times.

The retreat of the last ice sheet, about 12,000 years ago, left the surface appearance of Sutton much as it is today. As the climate improved, woodland began to cover the land, and by 5000 BC, when the rising seas swallowed up the land which had previously linked Britain to mainland Europe, the whole country was covered with woodland. At first the people who lived in England survived by hunting and gathering, and had few fixed settlements, but by 3000 BC agriculture was beginning to be established. This has been deduced from studies of the pollen found in silt deposits, which can be precisely dated, showing a decline in tree pollen, especially elm, and an increase in the pollen of weeds associated with agriculture. Herds of

Heathland in Sutton Park.

grazing animals prevented the regeneration of woodland, and clearances were made for growing crops, processes which, by 1000 BC, had resulted in tracts of heathland such as we see today in Sutton Park, and a landscape already tamed and formed by the activities of Man.

Although there have been no pollen studies in Sutton, traces left by these early inhabitants are still being found by archaeological search. Flint fragments from tools used by the hunter-gatherers have been found on the surface of ploughed fields, and, from a later period, flint and a stone axe used in the Neolithic period by Sutton's first farmers. Accumulations of heat-shattered stones dating back to the Bronze Age show where water was heated. It was once thought that these burnt mounds were Stone Age cooking sites, but the lack of any remains that would be expected at a site used for preparing food cast doubt on this, and a different interpretation is now favoured. The heated stones were placed in a shallow pit in a hut or tent, and water was then poured over them; people would then be able to enjoy a steam bath or sauna. The mounds accumulated over a long period of time, showing that the sites were either associated with settlements, or were returned to again and again if the people were travelling with their herds. They also show a level of organisation and routine which gives the lie to the assertion that prehistoric lives were nasty, brutish and short. Several such mounds have been found in Sutton; doubtless many more existed which have been obscured by development or are as yet unrecognised.

There are two burnt mounds near Langley Mill Farm, one to the south on Langley Brook and one to the north on Collets Brook. Both were recorded in 2001 during the archaeological survey carried out prior to the construction of the toll motorway. Between these sites, a little to the north-west of the farm, were found traces of the earliest settlement yet identified in Sutton (see opposite). The survey used the methods of fieldwalking (looking on the surface of ploughed fields for fragments of pottery, flint, etc.), analysis of aerial photographs, and resistivity (an electronic method of identifying structures below the ground surface). In a large field where fieldwalking had produced no fragments to indicate a settlement site, some resistivity anomalies were investigated by excavation. When the topsoil was removed, patterns of shallow ditches and post-holes were revealed, which were interpreted as an Iron Age farmstead that lasted from the second century BC to the first century AD, with several hut circles. This was succeeded by a Roman farmstead of the second and third centuries. Finds of Roman pottery and a quern-stone confirmed the date. Boundary ditches showed that a system of fields was associated with the settlement. A group of

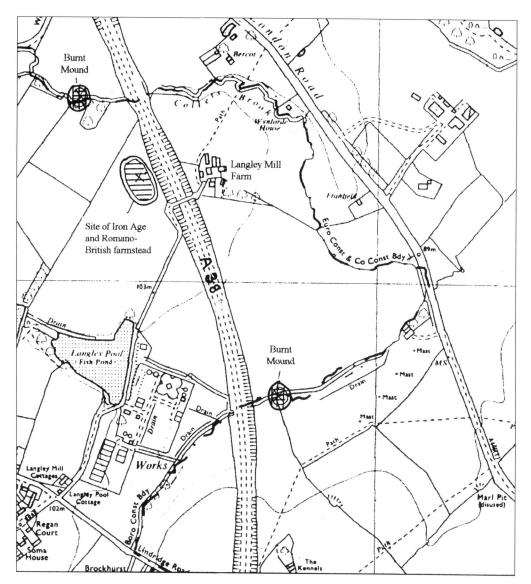

Map showing the location of the archaeological sites on the route of the M6 toll motorway.

ring ditches, probably related to burials, was found to the south of Langley Brook. No building stones or tiles were found, so the buildings would have been made of timber, clay and thatch, and would not have been of very high status.

This discovery adds to the growing evidence that Sutton was being fully exploited by Roman times, with the land being as extensively cultivated then as it was to be in 1320, the high point of the Middle Ages, with a correspondingly high population of about 1,500 inhabitants. In a study of Hanbury, a parish near Bromsgrove in Worcestershire, archaeological fieldwalking was extensively used to determine past levels and patterns of settlement; Hanbury was described as being in a 'Woodland Landscape', a landscape or *pays* extending over north Worcestershire, north Warwickshire and south Staffordshire. The research showed that Hanbury was at least as fully settled and farmed in Roman times as it was at the height of the Middle Ages, so raising the probability that other parishes in the same *pays* would also have been fully settled in Roman times.

Fieldwalking (see note on page 12) in Sutton, currently being undertaken by the Birmingham & Warwickshire Archaeological society, has produced a large number of fragments of Roman pottery. This is a clear sign that the land was being cultivated in Roman times, and indicates that other Roman farmsteads existed in addition to the one recorded in 2001 (for which fieldwalking had produced no evidence at all). During the 400 years of Roman occupation the province of Britain maintained a standing army of about 50,000 men, with a civil service of the same magnitude. To keep these forces supplied, heavy taxes were levied, often paid in the form of grain or other produce. The farming population was under great pressure to produce a surplus, which they did by taking in marginal land and increasing productivity. In addition, markets were well organised and thriving, giving a good return if additional farm products could be sold there. The Roman settlements at Metchley on Icknield Street (near the University of Birmingham at Selly Oak) and at Mancetter (on Watling Street near Grendon), and the more extensive one at Wall, the junction of these two Roman roads near Shenstone, would have provided ready markets locally. There may also have been other market towns in the Roman period which have not been identified, as well as other settlements such as the Roman villa at Coleshill, only excavated in 1978–9.

The discovery of a Roman pottery kiln in Sherifoot Lane near Mere Green in 1987 (found by accident during excavations for a garden pond) adds to the picture of a well-settled landscape. The kiln, dating from about AD 200, has been interpreted as a rural industry rather than as part of a larger settlement, but it must have been sited where there was easy access to a market for its products. Some of the pottery fragments found at the Langley Mill Farm site were from pots made at the Sherifoot Lane kiln. A very well-preserved stretch of Roman road can be seen in Sutton Park, where no doubt the landscape of moorland, marsh and thin woodland was much the same at the time of its construction (about AD 50) as it is today. Excavation has shown that the soil beneath

Above: The Sherifoot Lane Roman pottery kiln, showing the stokehole in the foreground and the flue and firing chamber beyond.
Right: Detail of the kiln, showing the pedestals that supported a clay floor where the pots were stacked.

The Roman road (Icknield Street) in Sutton Park.

At Keepers
Quarry in Sutton
Park the podzol
soil profile is
exposed – a thin
humus layer full
of roots overlies
the barren sand,
which is above
a slightly darker
layer (pan), a soil
type common in
heathland.

the road is a *podzol*, or heathland soil. But the rest of Sutton, once thought to have
been equally barren of settlement in Roman times, presented a very different picture
– as a fully settled and exploited landscape.

Following the withdrawal of the Roman army from England early in AD 410,
and the subsequent collapse of the Roman Empire, the markets declined and
agriculture reverted to subsistence farming. Although there is widespread evidence
for the abandonment of Roman settlements in the fifth century, a corresponding
abandonment of the agricultural land probably did not occur. Evidence for
continuity of cultivation has been found in the analysis of pollen grains in silt and
peat deposits datable to this period; no great increase in tree pollen or decline in
pollen of plants associated with agriculture has been detected. The inference is that
later settlers cultivated the same land as the Romans but did not occupy the same
settlement sites.

However, the cultivation of land at this time was less intensive, probably as a result
of the decline in population levels after the civil wars that broke out early in the fifth
century and the disastrous plague in the middle of the sixth century. Anglo-Saxon
colonisation had begun before the plague of AD 549 but progressed very rapidly after
it. Kinship was important to the Anglo-Saxons, replacing the tribalism of the British,
resulting in the formation of groupings of family units under *thanes* or sub-kings. It
has been suggested that the estates of early Anglo-Saxon sub-kings would have been

about 20 square miles in area. Such estates may well have been taken over from the British more or less intact, and may even have been land-holding units before Roman times. Sutton Coldfield has an area of approximately 20 square miles, as do a number of neighbouring parishes, so perhaps the origins of Sutton should be referred back to the Celtic settlers of the Iron Age.

In Roman Britain a grid pattern of small square fields had been imposed on the landscape, but such fields did not suit the heavier Anglo-Saxon plough, capable of turning the sod completely over. This plough was drawn by a team of eight oxen in four yokes; turning it at the end of a furrow was a cumbersome business, so the fields of Anglo-Saxon times tended to be very large to accommodate the furlong (220 yards, 200 metres) sweeps of the plough. These large fields were cultivated by several households, each perhaps supplying a yoke of oxen to the team, and the ploughing required cooperative effort if the whole field were to be ploughed in the same season. Rather than exhaust the soil fertility by cropping the field every year, additional large fields were established so that a rotation of different crops and a fallow period would maintain fertility.

Schematic plan of an open field system, loosely based on medieval Little Sutton. The plan shows a possible distribution of seventeen 1-acre strips or selions, sufficient for a subsistence farm. Strips were oriented to take advantage of the sloping land; water would drain away down the long furrows to a ditch at the bottom. Each open field was named; the names given here were the ones in use at Little Sutton in the sixteenth century.

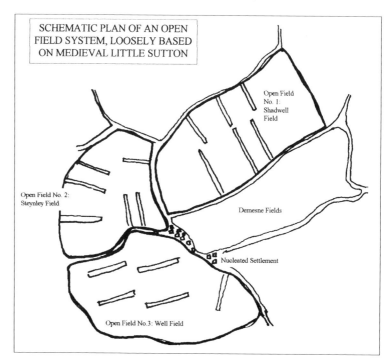

SCHEMATIC PLAN OF AN OPEN FIELD SYSTEM, LOOSELY BASED ON MEDIEVAL LITTLE SUTTON

Open Field No. 1: Shadwell Field

Open Field No. 2: Steynley Field

Demesne Fields

Nucleated Settlement

Open Field No.3: Well Field

Each field system was worked by a community of households whose members had to agree about the daily agricultural tasks in the fields they farmed. It appears that the farmsteads were usually scattered around the cultivated land, up to half a mile apart. By the tenth century a process of nucleation, where all the farms and cottages concerned with a field system were grouped together, often round a village green, at the heart of the field system, was well advanced. Some communities did not nucleate, but remained scattered, as seems to have been the case in Erdington and Perry Barr, but the communities in Sutton were all nucleated by the time of the Norman Conquest. Wigginshill and Greaves, a settlement that was not properly nucleated, was not part of Sutton until after 1086.

Although there is no proof that Sutton continued to be a settled agricultural area during the Anglo-Saxon period, circumstantial evidence indicates that it was. Some historians have speculated that it was a forested wasteland good only for hunting, but by working forwards from the Roman period, and backwards in time from the Normans, the more or less continuous cultivation of the arable areas seems the most likely interpretation. Archaeological techniques such as pollen analysis and fieldwalking generally indicate the continuity of agriculture. The name Sutton (derived from 'South Town') is Saxon, indicating a settlement established by people who were originally based to the north (Lichfield, Tamworth and Shenstone have all been suggested). With the growth in the English economy in terms of population and markets in the two centuries before the Norman Conquest, a market may well have been established at Sutton. Markets tended to be not more than 8 miles apart, so farmers would not need to travel more than 4 miles to their nearest market, and Sutton is about 8 miles away from the neighbouring market towns. The Normans found the manor of Sutton a more populous and thriving place than has sometimes been supposed.

Note – Fieldwalking. A group of people systematically searches the surface of a ploughed field for fragments of pottery or other man-made items. From earliest times it has been the practice to spread manure and farmyard rubbish over the land to improve fertility, and broken pots would be included in this rubbish. So if a scatter of Roman pottery is found in a field, the presumption is that it was cultivated land in Roman times. If there is a concentration of pottery, this would be a good indication of a settlement site.

TWO

Sutton in 1086

T he first historical record relating to Sutton Coldfield is found in the Domesday Book of 1086, a survey made for William the Conqueror to list the taxable resources of every town and village in England. Although the Domesday record appears to be a series of simple factual statements, the precise meaning of almost every item is difficult to prove, and it seems likely that some apparently significant items were not recorded. Surveying commissioners made assessments for each manor, and were organised into seven circuits covering different regions of the country. Warwickshire was in Circuit IV along with Leicestershire, Northamptonshire, Oxfordshire and possibly Staffordshire. The method of recording varied slightly from circuit to circuit. The Warwickshire section begins with a list of the overlords or tenants-in-chief with estates in the county, followed by an account of the manors owned directly by the Crown. Of over 350 entries for the county, nine were royal manors.

The Sutton entry begins by telling us about the lord of the manor: 'The King holds Sutone. Earl Edwin held it.' In the feudal system, tenants and peasants held their land from the lord of the manor in return for *services* such as working on the lord's land and maintaining ditches and banks. The lord held his manor from an overlord in return for services that may have been military. The overlord held his estates from the king in return for services in matters of state. There could be other links in the chain, or stages could be left out, as in the case of Sutton, where the lord of the manor was the king himself. Before the Norman Conquest Edwin the Earl of Mercia had also held Sutton directly, with no intervening steps of the hierarchy. The explanation for this royal interest in Sutton probably lies in the fact that the Manor House at Sutton served as a hunting lodge from which the surrounding areas of royal forest

The first page of the Warwickshire section of the Domesday Book. The tenants-in-chief are listed at the bottom of the left-hand column, while the right-hand column lists the king's manors, beginning with *Rex* ('the king').

and chase could be exploited and conserved. The Manor of Sutton would have been administered by royal officials: a bailiff to see that the lord's feudal interests were upheld and to manage the estate, and higher officials to represent the lord in the courts and to be responsible for the part of the forest called Sutton Chase.

The entry for Sutton continues: 'There are eight and a quarter hides and there is arable land for twenty-two ploughs.' Here the meaning is obscure since the hides approximate to 1,000 acres while the 22 ploughlands indicate over 2,000 acres of arable land. Possibly the hide, the old Anglo-Saxon assessment, may have been out of date; perhaps more land had since been brought under the plough, and the 22 ploughlands more accurately reflect the situation in 1086. The general growth of the later Anglo-Saxon economy, supported by evidence for the existence of several field systems in Sutton Coldfield by 1086, favours the higher figure. Estates belonging to powerful magnates seem to have been at the forefront of more intensive development, and, according to D. Hooke and S. Burnell in *Landscape and Settlement in Britain* (1995), 'some of the earliest signs of settlement planning seem to appear on royal estates', so perhaps the Earl of Mercia had been maximising his income from Sutton Coldfield by bringing more land under the plough.

Working backwards from later sources, it is possible to identify four field systems in the Manor of Sutton Coldfield which would amount to about 2,000 acres in total. These were at Maney, Great Sutton, Little Sutton and Hill. The communities that worked these fields lived in nucleated villages, at Great Sutton in the original Anglo-Saxon *burh* where the parish church now stands, and at Maney and Little Sutton in houses bordering a village green. At Hill, however, the settlement pattern has the appearance of being systematically planned. The houses were set out at regularly spaced intervals along both sides of the road leading to Lichfield, and each was provided with a plot of land of about an acre. Lanes led between these plots to the three open fields, giving a much more regular layout than the more haphazard pattern at Little Sutton, so perhaps the village of Hill is an early example of settlement planning. One of the Saxon Earls of Mercia may have developed the village and its fields on vacant land, or reorganised existing pioneer plots, thereby boosting the number of ploughlands above the old hidage rating.

The next line of the entry appears to give the population of Sutton at the time: 'There is one plough in demesne [that is, land farmed directly by the manor] and two servants; there are 20 villeins and four bordars with seven ploughs.' But this is also problematical. If there are 22 ploughlands, why are there only eight ploughs? A possible answer has been found by comparing the Domesday entries with the records of Burton Abbey (at Burton-on-Trent, 20 miles north of Sutton) dating from 1114 and 1126, and which relate to manors in Staffordshire and Leicestershire. These show that similar discrepancies in the Domesday Record for some manors, showing insufficient ploughs, were resolved in the slightly later record. In some manors all the

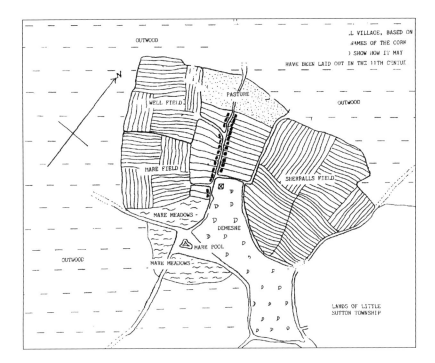

Schematic map of Hill village, based on the roads and field names of the Corn Rent map of 1824, to show how it may have been laid out in the eleventh century.

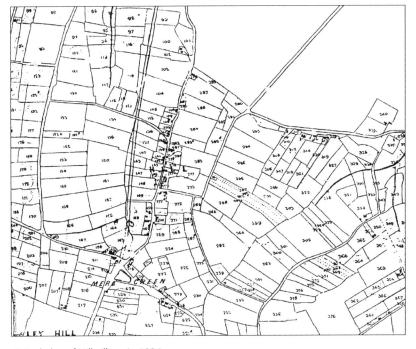

Actual plan of Hill village in 1824.

View across Sherrals Field today – the removal of hedges has returned the landscape nearly to its open field appearance.

'missing' ploughs were accounted for; they proved to belong to tenants paying their rent in money (*censarii*), whereas the 'Domesday' ploughs all belonged to customary tenants who rendered services for their land. These manors were in the same *pays* (the north Warwickshire and south Staffordshire woodland landscape) as Sutton, so it is reasonable to suppose that Sutton's missing fourteen ploughs also belonged to unrecorded money-renters. This is a crucial issue, since the households mentioned in

Ditch and bank boundary at Sherralls Field (near Hillwood Road).

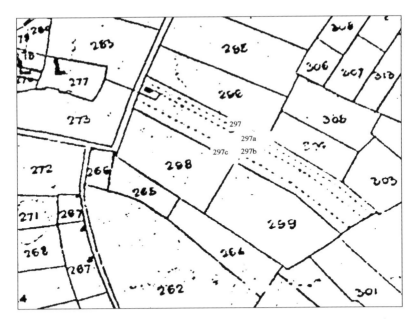

Detail of the Corn Rent map near Sherifoot Lane, showing 'Longlands'. These four unfenced strips are a relic of the old open field; at 400 yards long they are double the normal length but have the standard width of 11 yards, except 297b which was 22 yards wide. Presumably this was originally two strips. In 1824 the four strips were in the hands of four different owners, and in the occupation of four different farmers, each of whom owned or farmed other fields scattered across the three former open fields.

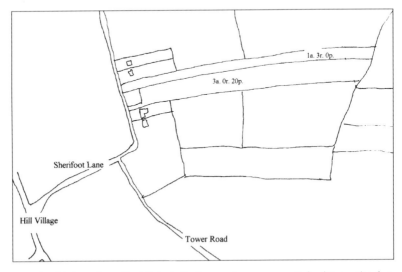

'Longlands', based on the 25-inch Ordnance Survey map, 3rd edition. The five original strips are now two long thin fields with an internal boundary hedge, the larger one being converted into allotment gardens when the Gibbons Road estate was developed. The surviving 'fossil' strips can still be seen, much overgrown with brambles and young trees.

'Longlands', the 'fossil' strip dating from the medieval open field, photographed in 1982 (left) and 2002.

Domesday total 26, giving a population of 130 using a household size of five people. On the basis of the proportion of missing ploughs, this represents only one-third of the probable total. If there were an even greater number of money-renters, giving sufficient households to allow four for each ploughland, the population figure would have been nearer 500. This figure is consistent with the other arguments put forward here; other histories of Sutton have generally given it as 130, which now seems unlikely.

The Domesday record continues: 'There are ten acres of meadow, woodland 2 leagues long and one league wide, and when it bears it is worth 30 shillings.' Assuming a league to be 1½ miles, this works out at 4½ square miles of woodland, or nearly 3,000 acres. This is considerably more than the arable acreage, being larger than the present-day Sutton Park, which is some 2,400 acres. If the total area of the Domesday manor of Sutton Coldfield was 12,000 acres (supposing its bounds to be much the same in the eleventh century as in the eighteenth), this woodland covered a quarter of the area. The woodland would be managed to produce both underwood and timber, which were important resources for building, fencing, firing, tools, implements, furniture, and so on. Another woodland product was charcoal, and there is some evidence for the production of charcoal in the Sutton area, but not on a large enough scale to support the suggestion that the name Coldfield meant field where charcoal was made. The management of the woodland probably involved regular coppicing, the underwood being felled every six or seven years, leaving some trees to mature until felled for timber. For the woodland to regenerate, they needed to be fenced to control the access of grazing animals. Not all the woodland was as intensively managed as this, and there seems to have been more than enough woodland to fulfil the needs of the inhabitants of Sutton.

The woodland products from the manor were an asset contributing to the wider economy of the lord, and could be sold to less well-endowed areas, thus accounting for the '30 shillings'. The phrase 'when it bears' probably refers to the rotational cropping of the underwood and timber, which may not have been done every year. An alternative interpretation sometimes given is that it refers to the crop of acorns for feeding pigs.

The woodland and farmland combined occupies over 5,000 acres, leaving another 7,000 acres unaccounted for. Most of this would be commons or waste land: heath, rough pasture, marshland and wood-pasture. This provided rough grazing for domestic and draught animals to supplement the relatively small area of hay-meadow. There may have been other areas of settlement, for example at Ashfurlong and Walmley, but a later date for these seems more likely.

The final part of the record states: 'The whole manor was and is worth four pounds.' There are over 350 manors in the Warwickshire section of Domesday Book, and most of them conclude with a statement of the value of the manor as it was before the Conquest and as it was in 1086. Birmingham, with four hides, was valued at 20s, while Aston, with eight hides, was worth £5, and Erdington, with three hides, 30s. The significance of this valuation is obscure, as we do not know how the figure was calculated. The entry for Aston includes a mill and a priest. Sutton probably had both of these, but they were not recorded.

The Domesday Book appears to record the basic pattern of settlement in Sutton Coldfield which was still in evidence in 1800, with its nucleated settlements at Hill, Little Sutton, Maney and Great Sutton and its extensive commons. Further details of the state of Sutton in 1086 can also be inferred from other sources. For example, land at Hill and Little Sutton was granted to Canwell Priory by the Earl of Warwick in about 1130, proving that these places existed then. Sutton was given by King Henry I to the Earl of Warwick in 1126 in return for the manor of Oakham in Rutland, and the document confirming the exchange gives details of some of the manor's assets. Roger de Newburgh, Earl of Warwick, could have the manor free of interference, with his own manorial court and view of frankpledge. There were two ploughlands in his direct ownership (demesne), and there was also a mill, a park, a chase, an enclosed wood and eighteen fallow deer. The Manor House is not mentioned, but its remains have been studied and it proved to be a very substantial building with a walled courtyard and gatehouse, and it included the Free Chapel of St Blaise.

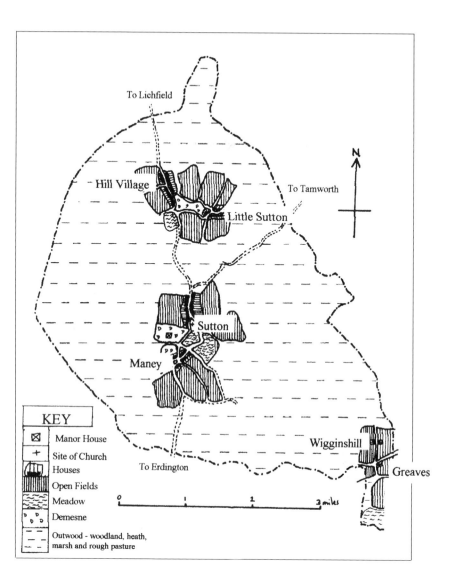

Map showing probable land use in Sutton Coldfield in 1086. This schematic plan is based on evidence from nineteenth-century field names and patterns, property deeds dating from the fourteenth to the nineteenth centuries, present-day landscape features and the Domesday Book.

No doubt the chapel was there at the time of Domesday, and the priest served the whole population of the manor. Where the Domesday Book can be checked against other sources, significant under-recording of churches has been found. In Kent there are known to have been over 400 churches with priests in 1086, but only 186 are listed in Domesday. Many of the unrecorded churches were in the Weald, a woodland *pays* similar to that of Sutton. Historians have supposed Sutton to have been a place of no account because no priest is recorded; this illustrates the danger of assuming that because it was not recorded, it did not exist. The same is probably true of the mill, which occupied a site just below Lower Parade, and the fenced woodland – all these assets were probably there before 1066.

The Earls of Mercia probably regarded Sutton Coldfield as a place of recreation, and certainly they used their Manor House as a hunting lodge. One Norman innovation was the introduction of the fallow deer as their favourite game animal, and with the deer came a whole host of laws and regulations for their protection and conservation. By arbitrary act William the Conqueror created over sixty forests in England, large tracts of land where forest laws protected the beasts of the chase.

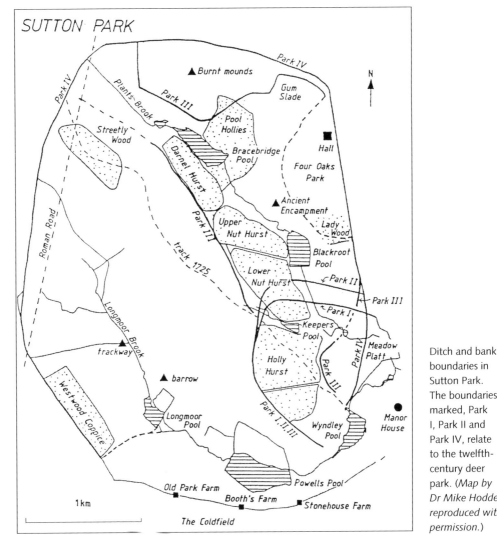

Ditch and bank boundaries in Sutton Park. The boundaries marked, Park I, Park II and Park IV, relate to the twelfth-century deer park. (*Map by Dr Mike Hodder reproduced with permission.*)

Part of the surviving deer park boundary (Park II) in Sutton Park.

William was a ferocious and energetic man, and hunting was one of his passions – and poachers had to beware. One of his royal forests was Kank, extending from the Tame to the Trent and including many villages with their open fields as well as woodland, heath and waste. Part of this forest, the chase of Sutton Coldfield, was given to the Earl of Warwick in 1126.

The same rules applied to the chase as to the forest, except that they were enforced by the earl rather than the king. Apart from the importance of the chase for the recreation of the aristocracy, the supply of venison to the earl and his relations was very important. Only a privileged few had access to venison, and no doubt the exclusivity of the dish was as important as its taste. The large chase was good for hunting, but so extensive that the deer could not always be quickly located, making it difficult for the hunters to guarantee a supply of venison to the nobleman's household at short notice. Deer parks were established (a royal deer park at Woodstock is supposed to have been the first, created in 1100 by Henry I) to conserve the deer so that they would increase more readily and be easier to catch when needed. The deer park at Sutton was in existence by 1126 and the remains of its ditch and bank boundary can be seen today along the western edge of Sutton Park. Similar boundary banks enclosing a smaller park within the larger one have also been identified.

In 1086 Wigginshill was a separate manor, but by 1126 it had been merged with Sutton to form part of the earl's manor. Wigginshill had a field system farmed by a small community split between the two tiny hamlets of Wigginshill (in Wigginshill Lane) and Greaves (known as Minworth Greaves, near the junction of Wigginshill Lane and Kingsbury Road). When the half-yearly view of frankpledge took place, every head of household was bound to renew his or her oath of fealty, and this they did through their *tithingman*. Each tithingman was responsible for ten households of this kind, and in Sutton there were ten tithings, organised so that the five administrative areas of Sutton each had two. These areas were called quarters (see note below), and Wigginshill was included in a quarter called 'Beyond the Wood', showing that it was very small in comparison to Sutton. Also included in this quarter was Walmley, but no open fields that could have been associated with Walmley in the eleventh century have yet been identified.

Apart from manorial employees working to maintain the chase, the park, and the Manor House, most people in Sutton worked on the land, producing the bread and ale which formed their staple diet. A document of 1308 gives an account of the rights and duties of the inhabitants, referring to those who held a yardland (about 32 acres) as eligible to be constables, while those who held only half a yardland (16 acres, a subsistence farm) could not hold offices above tithingman. These officials were chosen afresh each year, the constable being a supervisor over the tithingmen. Tenants held their land for life in return for services which included two days' work on the lord's land in the autumn (very light compared with other manors) and carrying out a range of duties in connection with hunting. Hunting was a complex business, requiring an army of beaters and other workers to make sure that the huntsmen would have something to shoot at, and this could be a very onerous duty if the earl and his friends were at leisure for any length of time. The lord was entitled to a share of the assets of inhabitants when they died, and when his eldest son was to be married. Householders were allowed to help themselves to wood for repairing their houses and hedges, and for fuel. Even with these relatively light duties almost everybody in Sutton had converted these services into a money rent by 1308 (many of them had done so by 1086). The 'typical' feudal peasant, a customary tenant farming 16 acres in return for services to the lord, was an exception in Sutton. Aspects of the feudal system were still important, however, and the lord kept a strong hold over his tenants as well as over his bondsmen.

Note – Quarters. The evidence for the Quarters comes later in the Middle Ages, for example in the Court Roll of 1416; it is presumed that the system was already in place in 1086, but this is purely speculation.

THREE

Medieval Expansion

The basic features of medieval Sutton were in place by 1086, but time brought changes. Although the national history is full of war and rebellion throughout the twelfth and thirteenth centuries, they were also centuries of growth in population and economy. The population growth meant that more and more people needed land to farm, and economic growth meant that there was a ready market for surplus produce. In these times, the Earls of Warwick sought to increase their revenue from their Sutton Coldfield Manor while retaining their valuable hunting grounds in the chase and park.

One way of winning friends and rewarding retainers was to grant them privileges, for example by allowing neighbouring lords to establish deer parks in their manors even though they were within the bounds of the chase. The lords of Shenstone, Weeford, Hints, Drayton Bassett, Middleton and Great Barr were all granted parks, and the lord of Perry was allowed to convert Perry Wood to agricultural uses. Greater favour was shown to the Arden family and the De Berefords, who were granted estates in Sutton Coldfield at Peddimore and Langley. Peddimore Hall and Langley Hall were both built in the thirteenth century and both had a moat, an essential status symbol at the time. The De Berefords of Wishaw rose in fame and fortune, William becoming Chief Justice of the Common Pleas in 1289, and Edmund De Bereford obtained a licence to crenellate Langley (that is, turn it into a castle) in 1327. These estates were established in the outwood or waste lands of Sutton, with only a few acres of land attached, but both families took part in another process, *assarting*.

In order to increase production it was necessary to bring more land into cultivation, but the forest laws in force in Sutton Chase forbade the clearing of land for cultivation.

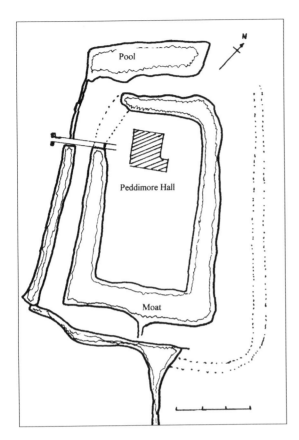

Left: Plan of the moat at Peddimore Hall. The large house platform is surrounded by a substantial moat, and there appear to be traces of another, outer, moat, represented by the duck pond to the north, the channel to the west and a depression to the east, but these features may originally have been fishponds and drainage channels.
Below: The eastern arm of the moat at Peddimore Hall.

The offence was called assarting. This apparent problem was turned to advantage by treating it as a legal fiction – assarts were made and the forest court duly punished the perpetrators with fines, and then confirmed the assart. This gave the assarter a legal title to his new land enshrined in the rolls of the forest court, while the lord received payment through the fine and an annual rent. Some means of compensating neighbours for the loss of land where they had grazing rights was also required, but in general the supposedly illegal process was to everyone's advantage. Large areas of Sutton, probably over 1,000 acres and perhaps as much as 2,000 acres, were brought into cultivation in this way between 1150 and 1300. Some of the earliest Sutton property deeds relate to assarts being made at Ramshurst, on the south side of Bulls Lane. The Warwick Castle Cartulary includes a copy of a charter of 1240 confirming assarts over a wide area, including the land between Bulls Lane and Ox Leys Road, an area known as *Burhale* said to lie between the two great roads leading towards Langley. In 1240 the Earl of Warwick granted to the Ardens of Peddimore the right to assart at the Sutton measure of 20 acres, with ditch and bank boundaries such that does with their fawns could leap over them. A recent archaeological survey in the area has found traces of just such boundary features.

Some of the assarting was carried out by the De Berefords and the Ardens, partly to add more farmland to their own estates and partly to rent out to other farmers, and sometimes large tracts of 40 acres were taken in at once. The process was also carried out on a lesser scale by the lesser gentry and yeomen. It was done in response to the demand for more produce for the increasing population, and the increased population provided the extra labourers and farm workers to clear and work the land. Although the same heavy ploughs and ox-teams were used in the new fields, which were usually big enough to allow for the plough to go 200 yards before turning, the new land was not organised into open fields with nucleated villages. In a few cases, as at Wylde Green Farm, a farmhouse was built on the new farmland with cottages for farm servants and labourers, but often the new land was simply added to existing farms. Some new settlements grew up, as at Four Oaks, Ley Hill, Hill Hook, Roughley, Reddicap Heath, Wylde Green, Over Green, Walmley Ash, Thimble End and Grove End. Most were very small, little more than a collection of labourers' cottages. The four last-mentioned, on the borders of the neighbouring manors of Wishaw and Minworth, were associated with substantial houses. There are two moated sites at Over Green, a substantial farm at Grove End, and a moated site at Walmley. At the first two of these the neighbouring settlement

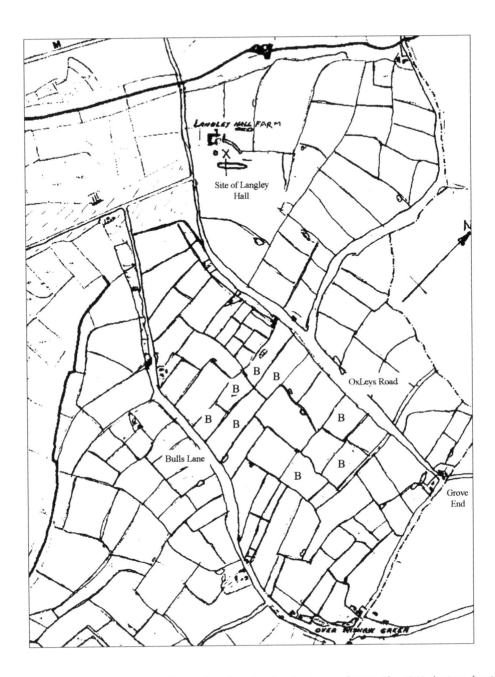

Plan of the area south of Langley Hall Farm, based on the Corn Rent map of 1824. The 1260 charter refers to 'two great roads leading towards Langley', now known as Bulls Lane and Ox Leys Road; the map shows their great width – over 50 metres in places. Roads through woodland were often given very wide verges to help protect travellers from the risk of ambush by outlaws. The roads are said to lead towards Langley, as though this was the normal direction of approach rather than from Sutton. The manor of Wishaw also belonged to the De Berefords and this would also be the approach to Langley from Warwick. The land between the two roads was referred to as Burhale; the Corn Rent map schedule of 1824 names all the fields, and those marked here with a 'B' contain the word 'Burrells' – undoubtedly a corruption of the medieval *Burhale*.

Right: Looking across the fields from Bulls Lane; the distant buildings are on Ox Leys Road. The hedgerows crossing the shallow valley were set out in 1240 to define newly assarted fields, the slightly curving boundaries corresponding to the aratral curve created by the medieval plough.

Below: The moated site at Walmley on the corner of Webster Way.

has all but disappeared, but at Walmley Ash the moated site was deserted while the hamlet continued to flourish. By 1320 the population of Sutton had increased to nearly 1,500. This estimate is not entirely guesswork; a list of the taxpayers for a tax levied in 1327, known as the Lay Subsidy Roll, records 69 names in Sutton Coldfield. About 5 per cent of the population were taxpayers, so the names represent a population of the order of 1,400.

The Earl of Warwick was the lord of many manors, and his numerous officers and retainers made sure that his estates were properly managed and fully exploited to maximise his income. Throughout the twelfth and thirteenth centuries hunting in the chase and venison from the park continued to be important to the lord, but the manorial property in Sutton, the demesne, was also developed. A *vaccary* (dairy farm) was established near the manor house, which also had a dovecote. Fisheries were improved and new ones established at Wyndley Pool, Keepers Pool and perhaps the Mill Pool. The mill pool was formed by the building of a causeway across the valley bottom (now The Parade). As well as giving better access to Sutton and Maney than the alternative route via Clifton Road, this improved the head of water to give more power to the mill and converted swampy unproductive marshland into a productive fishery. The mill was an especially valuable asset since the customs of the manor required all the corn grown in Sutton to be ground at the lord's corn mill, giving him a monopoly. The miller took a toll (or percentage) of all the flour ground as payment for his work, and the lord received a substantial annual rent, or 'farm', from the miller, who contributed about one-tenth of the total income from the manor. The watermill was the principal mill in Sutton. There may also have been windmills at Maney Hill and near Langley Mill Farm, but they have left no trace.

An important aspect of the role of feudal lords was display – they were expected to show off their wealth and power by having a large retinue and a handsome house as well as excelling in the hunt and martial activities. In the twelfth century an important status symbol was the impressive moat encircling a hall or manor house. However, the old Sutton Manor House on the hill did not have a moat. This difficulty was overcome by building a new hall with a moat to serve as the hunting lodge, and this was named simply 'New Hall'. The site must have been part of the demesne property in Sutton, probably within the enclosed woodland referred to in the 1126 Exchange Charter. This demesne woodland may have occupied the whole of the New Hall Valley as far as Eachelhurst, an extent of about 600 acres, and was bounded by a ditch and bank, the remains of which survive at the side of Walmley

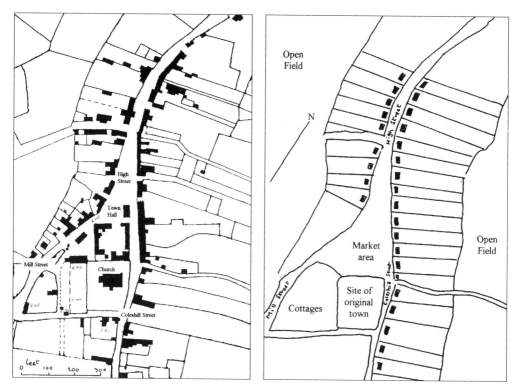

Above, left: Sutton town centre in 1824, redrawn from the Corn Rent map by the late Norman Evans. The substantial houses are north and east of the church in High Street and Coleshill Street, while the humbler dwellings are to the south and west. The triangular space north of the church was the market place, which included the ground floor of the town hall. The church and churchyard occupy a hill-top on a spur of high ground with a steep drop on three sides, presenting an ideal strategic site for the original Saxon settlement of South-tun.

Above, right: Hypothetical plan of Sutton as newly laid out in about 1200. The Saxon town, with its flimsy houses clustered within the defensible site on the hill-top, was abandoned in favour of more substantial timber-framed houses on High Street and Coleshill Street, with 40-ft frontages and a plot of land attached. This planned new town layout occupied the edges of the open fields, which previously extended to the edge of the streets, while the market area and the cottages had been open land near the town where the village herd would graze overnight.

Road. By 1300 most of the woodland to the south of New Hall had given place to farmland, while the remaining 200 acres formed the New Hall Estate.

The development of Sutton as a market town was as much in the lord's interest as fostering the growth of agriculture. The settlement known as Great Sutton, on top of the hill where the parish church now stands, was increasing in importance throughout the thirteenth century, and had a market and some specialised tradesmen long before the granting of a market charter in 1300. At some point, possibly around 1200, a new town area appears to have been laid out along High Street, with timber-framed buildings in regularly spaced house-plots. These had a frontage on the street and long gardens (burgage plots) behind, a feature of town planning in this period of expanding markets and growing towns. In the tenth and eleventh centuries houses had been of slight construction, with walls of woven hazel-rods. Later in the eleventh century more solid structures of posts and planks became prevalent, while timber-framed buildings came into favour about 1200. The old town area decayed, and the first parish church was built on the site, with a churchyard, and a resident parish priest was appointed. The construction date of the church is commonly given as 1291. The first documentary reference to it is in the ecclesiastical taxation records of this date, but an early thirteenth-century origin is more likely. Before the church was built the chaplain from the manor had provided for the spiritual needs of the population, probably in a makeshift converted building in Sutton rather than at the manor house chapel. The chaplain received a salary from the manorial income in addition to his wage as a member of the earl's household. The new parish church was endowed with a glebe (a small landed estate) by the Earl of Warwick. The priest was answerable to the Bishop of Lichfield, whereas the chaplain of the Free Chapel of St Blaise had been answerable to the Earl of Warwick (and before 1126 to the king and before 1066 to the Earl of Mercia).

The market charter of 1300 gave the finishing touch to the growth of Sutton over this period. Markets were held weekly in an open area at the junction of High Street, Mill

The stone plinth at the base of the chancel wall is probably thirteenth century.

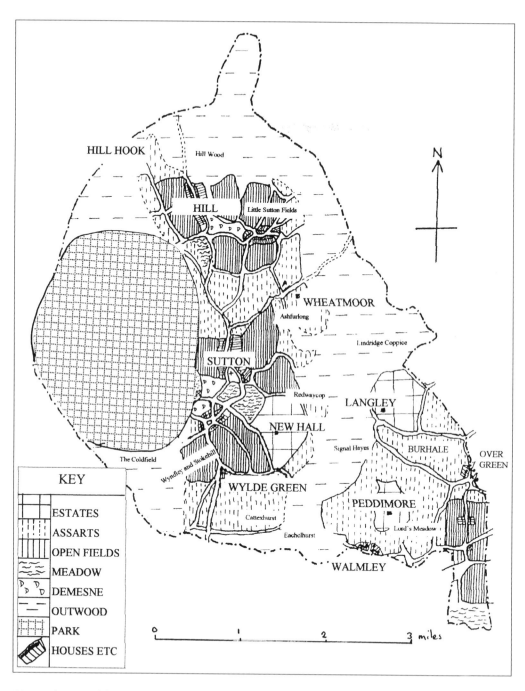

Map to show possible land use in Sutton, *c*. 1320.

Street and Coleshill Street, serving the local area up to 4 miles around and attracting trade from further afield. There was a tendency for market towns to be about 8 miles apart. Lichfield, Tamworth, Coleshill, Birmingham and Walsall were the neighbouring markets and all were about this distance from Sutton and from one another.

The basic network of roads used by people travelling to market in 1300 is largely still in existence, but the roads were only clearly defined where they passed through farmland; across the commons they would be unfenced tracks. Although the Birmingham to Lichfield route was the principal road in the town, the charter of 1240 granting assarts at Burhale shows the importance of other routes. It refers to 'two great roads leading towards Langley', that is, Bulls Lane and Ox Leys Road, which lead towards Langley not from Sutton but from Wishaw (a manor belonging to the De Berefords), and from the ancient road from Warwick and Coleshill. This would have been the route taken by the Earl of Warwick and other high-status visitors to Langley and Sutton. Early maps show them as very wide roads, over 100 feet across, through the area known as Sutton Woods; wide clearings were usually made on both sides of roads through woodland to reduce the risk of being ambushed by outlaws. Roads were commonly used for driving cattle and sheep to market or to pasture, and sometimes had wide verges, but farmland was protected by a substantial ditch and bank with a hedge or fence to prevent animals straying on to the crops. The manorial courts fined anyone who failed to maintain the section of hedge for which he was responsible, and also ordered the roads to be maintained, usually by clearing rubbish and debris, but sometimes giving orders for the repair of a ford or the making of a bridge.

Since the Norman Conquest the area of farmland in Sutton had doubled and the population had trebled, both recovering to the levels previously achieved in Roman Britain. Much of the newly colonised land had probably been agricultural land in Roman times which had reverted to the wild, but not all the Roman fields were recolonised and some of the new land had never previously been cultivated. Some of the woodland had been cleared since 1086, but much remained. The name of the quarter 'Beyond the Woods' suggests that most of the woods were on the Keuper Marl soils to the east of the New Hall Valley, and some of the early assarting deeds refer to new intakes at Bulls Lane as being 'in Sutton Woods', but there was also woodland at Hill Wood and in Sutton Park. A striking feature of the Sutton scene was still the vast area of heath, marsh and rough grassland forming (excluding Sutton Park) over 5,000 acres of waste.

FOUR

Sutton in the Later Middle Ages

The flourishing state of Sutton in 1320, with its church, market, burgeoning town and expanding agriculture, was short-lived. In 1323 a robbery took place on a road called the Ridgeway (Chester Road near the Beggar's Bush), when £300 was stolen from Elias le Collier. This was a very large sum, and the authorities were determined that it should be recovered. When the crime remained unsolved the county in which the robbery took place was ordered to pay compensation for failing to prosecute. As the Ridgeway formed the boundary between Warwickshire and Staffordshire, the sheriffs of both counties were called upon to pay, but they pleaded that there was such a dearth and plague of cattle that the money could not be raised. This hardship of 1323 was one of a series of disasters that struck the country: cattle plague (probably foot-and-mouth disease), crop failures and famine, and then in 1348 the Black Death – bubonic plague. Within thirty years the population of England had been cut by two-thirds, and the population of Sutton was back to its 1086 level of about 500 from the estimated 1,500 of the year 1320.

The reduced population could not provide sufficient labour to cultivate the land, nor would there have been a market for the surplus had any been produced. Much of the arable land was converted to pasture, or reverted to common. The Earl of Warwick also had to adapt, which he did by leasing out his manor house and park, and establishing a new deer park at Eachelhurst. He moved his dairy farm to New Shipton, converting its 160 acres of arable land to pasture, and here he built a large timber-framed barn which is still standing. The barn is of cruck construction, each cruck being made from two halves

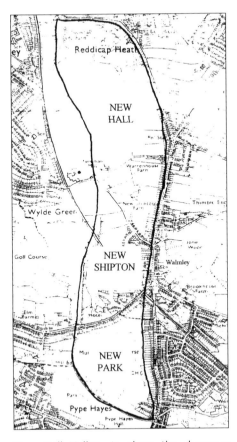

New Hall Valley, to show the demesne properties referred to in 1480. If New Hall is included, these demesne lands could comprise the enclosed wood which was part of the demesne in 1126.

of an oak tree split lengthways. Cores taken from the crucks which were analysed by tree-ring dating (dendrochronology) showed that the trees had been felled in 1425.

The tenant of the manor and park in 1419 was Ralph Bracebridge of Kingsbury, who paid an annual rent of £10 or 120 bream. A highly prized fresh-water fish, bream were used in the households of the great at times of fasting and abstinence. There is some evidence that the park was being managed to maximise the production of fish at this time, with the creation of Bracebridge Pool. There are traces at the side of Little Bracebridge Pool of ancient fish stews, small ponds where the fish fry were nurtured prior to their release into the main pool. Earthworks in the form of a bank and ditch survive which enclosed the whole of the Blackroot Valley, as if to keep unwanted animals and other intruders out of the area where the fish were being conserved and also to protect the woodland (see map on page 22: this boundary is 'Park III').

The feudal system was still in force, but most land was now held by rent rather than by service. The strips or selions of land in the open fields were held on a more flexible basis. At Wigginshill selions were being bought and sold, and between 1363 and 1367 Thomas Taylor of Maney was able to purchase twelve selions of land in Middle Maney Field. But the lord of the manor controlled all these dealings, and every new tenant had to pay his entry fine to the court. From the early fifteenth century onwards many of the court rolls for Sutton survive; these were the records of the various transactions of the half-yearly courts. The earliest known court roll for Sutton Coldfield dates from 1412, and it is one of a number of fifteenth-century court rolls in the Middleton Papers at Nottingham University. The earliest of these which is complete and fully legible is for 1416.

Interior of the barn at New Shipton, showing the cruck construction (crucks 3 and 4).

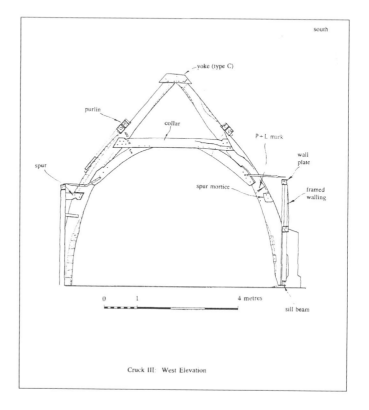

Elevation of Cruck 3 at New Shipton, from the survey by Oxford Archaeology.

Bracebridge Pool.

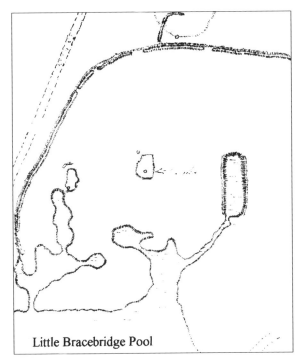

Little Bracebridge Pool

Sketch of the 'fish-stews' at Little Bracebridge Pool.

The court was also a view of frankpledge, at which all the heads of households were required to renew their oaths of allegiance to the Crown. The roll of 1416 also includes details of the small court where minor claims were heard. The lord of the manor often presided at his court, but the Earl of Warwick employed officials to do this for him in his many manors. Besides, in 1416 the earl was away in France; the battle of Agincourt had been fought and won the previous year and Warwick was given command of the army there after Henry V returned to England.

Fish stews, with Little Bracebridge Pool in the background.

A series of local officials reported to the court, beginning with the tithingmen for Great Sutton. Tithingmen, known locally as headboroughs or thirdbarrows, swore fealty on behalf of all the households in their locality. Theoretically, each tithingman represented ten households, but in practice each of the five quarters of Sutton had two tithingmen, regardless of differences in size, and they were chosen anew at each court. In 1416 they reported that two new households had entered the Great Sutton tithing. Every household had to belong to a tithing or else be outside the law (outlaws). In this way the Crown was able to account for the entire population of the country, since everybody was covered by their local manorial court.

Next came the tasters of bread and ale, who listed all the bakers and brewers and the amount of their fines. Although baking and brewing for resale was against the law, this was an artifice for making sure that good standards were maintained. The fine was effectively a licence fee, as was the fine levied on the miller. He was fined for keeping excessive toll (the miller was allowed to keep a proportion of the flour he ground as his payment) but this is probably a fiction, the real object being to record his name in the court roll as the certified miller for the manor.

Then followed reports of the officials for the other four quarters – Little Sutton, More and Ashfurlong, Wigginshill, Walmley, Maney and Wyndley. There were two fights to report in Wygynghull and Warmeley, as well as a bridge in poor repair, while blocked ditches were more of a problem at Maney. Then the jury was sworn in and Thomas Mason came to pay his entry fine of 8d for a selion in Sutton Open Field. All the officials reported that they had given alms to the poor – 21*d* in Great Sutton, 20*d*

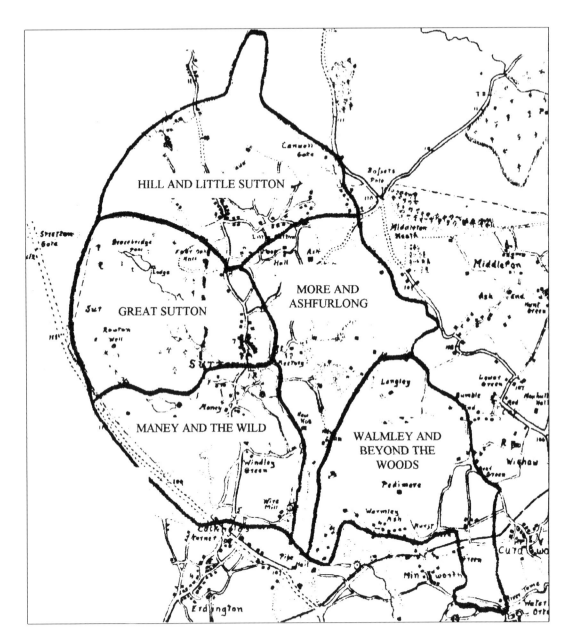

The quarters of Sutton, based on Yates's map of Warwickshire of 1789, as redrawn by the late N.G. Evans in 1979. The map shows the approximate boundaries of the five administrative units of Sutton as they were in 1789.

in Little Sutton, 10*d* in More and Ashfurlong, 10*d* in Wigginshill and Walmley, and 8*d* in Maney and Wyndley.

The lesser court dealt with pleas of trespass and debt, and most of the cases were carried forward to the next court. The court had powers to deal with infringements of the regulations of Sutton Chase; it received the report of one of the foresters, as a result of which an Erdington man was fined for selling 'fruits of the forest' at Coleshill. There followed some disputes about property, and a dispensation to the wealthiest inhabitants to be excused attendance at the courts. The proceeds of the court, £4 2s ½*d* formed part of the manorial income for the lord of the manor.

The court roll throws light on a number of issues. There was a net gain of households in the year, since five newcomers were sworn in while only three had gone. All three of those who left were from Walmley and Wigginshill quarter, an area where marginal land had been brought into cultivation in the thirteenth century. This and the report that some houses were in disrepair could be an indication of the reduced demand for resources following the Black Death. However, we know that some new buildings were being erected because they survive today, datable from their cruck construction and the age of their timber. The Old Smithy at Maney, Forge Farm in Walmley Ash, the barn at Minworth Greaves on Kingsbury Road and the house from Minworth Greaves that was moved to Bournville in 1911 all date from the fifteenth century; and no doubt there were others which have not survived. The areas where traditional open-field agriculture was the norm seem to be almost without incident. Little Sutton (including Hill), with a population as high as Great Sutton, has very little to report, only a dispute about hedges, but this may be a sign that the open field system was already being abandoned if it marks an attempt to privatise part of the open field.

Since every householder in Sutton owed suit to the court, and only a few are fined for absence, the court can be used to estimate the total population in broad terms. There are 127 names in the court roll; most of them were heads of households, and on average a household consisted of 5 persons, so the total population was probably between 500 and 700.

The Earl of Warwick, Richard Beauchamp, was a powerful and rich baron with an efficient household. It was the business of the earl's receiver general to make sure that each manor was operating efficiently, and to maximise its income. About the time of this court roll a particularly able receiver general, John Baysham, was active, so Sutton was certainly not neglected by its lord. Thus, although the market may have been reduced or in abeyance, there were quite a number of tradesmen. Of the sixteen people fined for brewing ale, nine were in Great Sutton – an indication that people from round about often had occasion to go into Sutton. Little Sutton, which may have been equally populous, with two nucleated settlements, had only four brewers. The scattered rural community of More and Ashfurlong reported no brewers at all.

Another indication of economic activity is the number of cases in the minor court. The eleven cases of debt show that money was circulating, and that people had sufficient confidence in their ability to repay. The hearing of debt cases in the minor court is more often a way of recording transactions than seeking immediate repayment. The seventeen cases of trespass also reflect an active community, as those with rights defended them against their careless or thrusting neighbours. The lord's interest in the affairs of Sutton is shown by his defence of manorial lands as well as by his active management of the chase. We know from the 1433 bailiff's account that fallow deer were being dispatched from Sutton to the Earl of Warwick, and here forest products are jealously guarded. In total these cases produced proceeds for the court of over £4, a considerable portion of the lord's income from the manor, which was about £50. The more active the courts, the more income they produced for the lord.

The nine ale-sellers in Great Sutton were, no doubt, busy on the day the court was held, as a good proportion of the population was assembled there. The social life of the town probably revolved around events such as the court, religious festivals and market days, helping to give the scattered population of Sutton a sense of community. Traders from further afield would bring news of local and national events to add to the local parish pump gossip, while the bailiffs and the clergy would give out official information. The court roll can only give us a glimpse of a complex web of people going about their daily business, making their living and enjoying their leisure.

A more lengthy Sutton document, the bailiff's account or *compotus* for 1433, is in the Stratford Record Office. This helps us to see Sutton from the viewpoint of the lord of the manor, Richard Beauchamp, Earl of Warwick. The ability, authority and fortunes of the successive lords, be they Saxon Earls of Mercia, Norman kings or Earls of Warwick, affected the life of the manor.

Only a part of the 1433 account survives. The first item, nearly £20, is for the assessed rents, and represents the payments for all the older houses and farmland in Sutton, excluding Hill and Little Sutton which were payable to Canwell Priory. There follows a list of increased rents paid by named individuals for specified land,

Part of the Bailiff's Account (*compotus*) of 1433 (reduced); the parchment is torn off at the bottom and there is a large hole in the centre.

for example: '1*d* new rent from John Penkrich for 1 piece of waste land next to Radwaycoppe containing half an acre of land as appears in the court rolls, this being the 33rd year.' One of these items is new rent for *Mullemoor* of 12*d* payable by Agnes Herman and her son John for the term of their lives; they are possibly ancestors of Bishop Vesey. These additional items would have accrued since the rent was last fully reassessed, which was probably done in about 1400, so these eleven new items worth 2*s* 3*d* show only very small growth over thirty-three years.

The next items, increased rents, show rather more growth. There are only four items but they are worth 7*s* 7*d*, including: '4*s* 4*d* increased rent for a messuage with half a yardland of arable in Mandy lately held by John Short, now demised for the term of their lives to Robert Osborne and his wife Agnes, over and above the 2*s* 4*d* old rent payable.' Half a yardland, 16 acres, was a subsistence plot, so this gives some idea of prices at the time. Next comes £4 6*s* 8*d* for the mill, which Robert Milward of Perry had leased since 1400, on condition that he keep it in good order; this mill still had the monopoly for grinding corn produced in the manor of Sutton.

In 1433 the manor house was vacant, but in previous years it had been demised to 'Ralph Bracebruge knight, with the herbage of the park for £10 per annum'. The Earl of Warwick's proctor, Matthew Smallwood, then had the farm of the park (that is, he kept all the income from grazing, sale of timber, fishing, etc.) at £7 6*s* 8*d* a year for twenty-one years, that being the tenth year, by deed under the seal of the Earl of Warwick dated 28 January 1 Hen. VI (1423), reserving sufficient grazing each year for the wild beasts there. This section, 'manorial income', relates to the lord's demesne. There is mention of five pools or fish ponds in the park, corresponding with the five pools mentioned by Leland in the next century when he recorded a tradition that their dams were rebuilt with great heads of stone by Richard Beauchamp the Earl of Warwick around 1415. (The pools were Wyndley, Keepers, Bracebridge, the town mill pool, and a pool near the present Youth Centre called Cross Pool.) The old dairy farm produced nothing, but the new one at New Shipton was let to John Verney for £4 12*s* 8*d*. John Verney was the Earl of Warwick's receiver general, so this must have been a good bargain and a prestigious property. There is reference to a dovecote 'destroyed by crows and weasels and other vermin', and to the Lords Meadow called Petymore, a meadow near Peddimore Hall which later formed the basis of the Lord's Meadow Charity. The rest of the account is torn off and missing, but the fate of the two carucates of land which formed part of the demesne in 1126 may be explained by a later account, which refers to 216 acres formerly let to various tenants for 18*s* 10*d* but now producing no income 'because all and singular the above mentioned land is included in the park there'. However, these 216 acres are equally likely to have been used in the creation of the new park at Eachelhurst. It seems impossible to identify where 216 acres of arable land could have been included in Sutton Park unless it was extended to the east, perhaps as far as Lichfield Road.

On the reverse of the account are the following items:

4 quarters and 2 bushells of tolcorn received for the livery of the palesman at a quarter per 12 weeks

total 4 quarters 2 bushells of the same for the livery of the said head palesman as above this year.

And for 11 quarters 3 bushels 1 peck of oats bought as below for the chase rider this year at the rate of a peck a day.

And for a pound of pepper due in rent at Christmas.

And for eight iron wedges carried forward from the previous year used by the park palesman for splitting wood. And for two saws and an iron file.

And for 3 eyries of swans brought forward from the previous year

And for 24 cartloads of hay brought forward from the previous year, and 23 cartloads produced by the meadows this year – total 47. Of which 20 cartloads were used for the lord's horses in the hunting season and 3 were the customary annual livery of the Chase Rider; and 24 cartloads remain in the grange.

And on another fragment:

the expenses of Robert Kelyng bailiff riding from Sutton to Caversham to present this account there from the 1st to the 6th October after the end of the accounting year – 3s 4d. And in supplying – Duffels clerk with hospitality at the expense of Robert Kelyng and 12s for carriage of 12 fat bucks from Sutton to the lord there this year.

These show the importance still attached to the park and the chase; there must have been a good deal of hunting if the horses ate twenty cart-loads of hay, and the earl evidently had a taste for venison. Bucks were hunted in the summer months when they were 'in grease', as were the twelve fat bucks in the account; these would have been salted and packed in barrels before being transported. Does were hunted in the winter months, which may be when the hay was consumed. There is no payment mentioned for the beaters and all the other assistants at the hunt, so perhaps these customary labour services were still being exacted. Hunting for sport may not have needed many hands, but if the huntsmen had to fill a specific order for the earl's household they probably used an army of beaters banging drums and blowing horns to scare the deer into nets or to drive them towards the waiting bowmen. No doubt the Sutton yeomen were skilled with the bow, and were called on for military service on occasion, but there is no record of this.

Most of the Earls of Warwick had been involved in warfare, and their changing fortunes had an effect on Sutton. Roger of Newburgh became Earl of Warwick in 1123 on the death of his father, who had been a good subject of King Henry I. Earl Roger made frequent journeys to the Holy Land and struggled to survive the civil wars of Stephen and Matilda. He was succeeded in 1153 by his son William who was loyal to Henry II, a king who was rarely out of the saddle, fighting battles on the few occasions when he was not hunting. He jealously exploited and conserved all his forests, and Earl William may have followed suit in exploiting Sutton chase. William died in the Holy Land in 1184 and was succeeded by his brother Waleran, who was plagued by an imposter's attempts to displace him, claiming to be his elder brother returned from Jerusalem. Waleran died in 1204 and his son Henry, a minor, became earl in 1213, supporting King John in his various battles in that turbulent reign. Henry was succeeded in 1228 by his son Thomas who died childless in 1242, leaving his sister Margery as countess. She was made to marry a favourite of King Henry III, John de Plessets, a soldier engaged in the Welsh wars and in the early skirmishes of the barons' wars. He was succeeded in 1263 by William Mauduit, the grandson of Waleran, who was taken prisoner in the barons' wars and died in 1267.

This brought a new dynasty to Warwick in the form of Mauduit's nephew, William de Beauchamp, who was already a powerful baron. He flourished under King Edward I, the 'Hammer of the Scots', and it was probably under this energetic and forceful earl that Sutton church was built, and due to his management that Sutton received its market charter two years after his death. He was succeeded in 1298 by the warlike Guy, whose energies were largely taken up in trying to survive the reign of King Edward II. His son Thomas became earl in about 1327, and held high office under King Edward III. Sutton was now at least being well governed in the bad times of the Black Death. Thomas was succeeded in 1369 by another Thomas, who was heavily involved in the Hundred Years War, taking 200 men at arms and 200 bowmen over to France with him in 1373. He was made Governor of England during the minority of King Richard II, being thought the most able of the barons. But Richard II threw off the old guard on his majority and installed his favourites, and Thomas ended up a prisoner on the Isle of Man. He recovered all his lands on the accession of King Henry IV, and died in 1401 having a great reputation for his 'Valour, publique spiritedness, Piety and Charity'. His restoration in 1399 may have been the occasion for consolidating the Sutton rental.

Thomas's son Richard was even more wealthy, powerful and renowned, early distinguishing himself in the king's service at the Battle of Shrewsbury. He journeyed to Jerusalem, winning fame at tournaments in France and Italy by unseating all comers, and came back through Russia, Poland and Germany performing deeds of derring-do against all the best knights of Europe. He fought in France with King Henry V, and was Governor of Calais from 1415 to 1417. By a series of advantageous marriages he doubled his estates and became the wealthiest baron in England. A few records of the management of his extensive estates survive, which show that his affairs were managed by a number of efficient officials, two of whom are mentioned in the Sutton *compotus* of 1433 – John Baysham and John Verney held the offices of receiver general and supervisor respectively. In 1422 Richard was asked to form the government in the new reign of the six-month-old King Henry VI, but he coped well with the challenge and remained at the height of his powers until his death in 1435. By contrast his son Henry was rather sickly and not very forceful; he died in 1445, making way for Richard Neville.

Richard Neville, son-in-law of Richard Beauchamp, became Earl of Warwick in 1445, and was soon campaigning on behalf of the Yorkist claim to the throne. He is said to have sold off vast quantities of Sutton Coldfield timber in the 1450s to help finance his military and political ambitions, leaving the town in an impoverished state. The first battle of the Wars of the Roses was fought at St Albans, when Warwick was on the losing Yorkist side, but King Henry's court transferred to Coventry because London was unsafe. In 1461 the Yorkists won the Battle of Towton and installed Edward IV on the throne. Warwick soon became disaffected. Raising an army in France, he invaded England, rescued Henry VI from the Tower of London and restored him to the throne. The next year King Edward IV won the Battle of Barnet and regained the throne. Warwick's death at Barnet was very bad for Sutton, because his manors were soon alienated to rapacious opportunists. But even when things had been going well for him he would bleed his manors dry to finance his campaigns.

In 1471 Sutton passed to the Duke of Clarence along with the rest of Warwick's estates, and a period of relative tranquillity followed. With the disgrace and death of Clarence in 1479 his estates reverted to the Crown. There is an account of the king's bailiff of Sutton Coldfield for 1480 in the Public Record Office. This document follows the 1433 account almost exactly. In making their accounts successive bailiffs simply copied the previous year's accounts unless there were any additional or reduced payments. There were not apparently very many changes in the forty-seven years between the two accounts. The 1480 account is complete, however, and shows how the town and chase gave the lord of the manor opportunities for patronage. New Shipton had been let to Richard Dey in 1455; a rich Coventry grazier, he was perhaps given the prestigious lease to retain his support. Richard Lee had the farm of the herbage of the park for £8 per annum, and Thomas Lesyng had the farm of the mill; the chaplaincy of the Chapel of St Blaise, with an income of £3 per annum at least, was also in the gift of the lord of the manor. But more important retainers held the offices connected with the chase and park.

These offices were: Keeper of the Park (60s 8d) Humfrey Gelson; Bailiff of Lynrich (45s 6d) John Golson; Bailiff of Hulwode (60s 8d) James Cayleh; Bailiff of the Collefeld (60s 8d) Roger Holden; Keeper of Berwode (60s 8d) John Knyght; Forest Rider of the chase of Sutton and Colvyle and Sutton Park (£5) William Berkeley Esq. After the fall of Warwick in 1471 Clarence would have given these sinecures to his own retainers, and when King Edward took over he replaced them with his own men. William Berkeley was Lord of the Manor of Weoley Castle, and no doubt the others were local gentry whose support the king wished to retain. There were some duties attached to these posts. The chase was administered in four sections, Hillwood in the north, Lindridge to the east, Berwood to the south and Coldfield to the west of Sutton, and the keeper or bailiff was responsible for preserving the game and supervising the hunting. In 1477 Willoughby of Middleton went hunting in Hillwood by permission of the keeper, with a party of sixty, but they were set upon by a hundred men of Lord Lisle of Drayton Bassett, who seemed to think the Bangley Woods were his preserve. Clearly it was not all plain sailing for the keepers.

The end of the Wars of the Roses and the accession of Henry VII in 1485 did not restore Sutton to its former thriving state. The depredations of the period left the market forsaken, the manor house dismantled (its materials were used in building Bradgate Park, Leicestershire), the woods destroyed and the people impoverished. An energetic lord would perhaps have been able to restore its prosperity, but Henry VII was not a king to spend any money if he could help it, and Sutton entered the new century in a poor state.

FIVE

Bishop Vesey

Three accounts of Sutton in the early sixteenth century all agree that the town was in a poor state. 'The Market being utterly forsaken, the Town fell much to ruin, and the Mannour place was totally pulled down . . . and in this decayed condition did Sutton continue.' So wrote Sir William Dugdale in 1656. According to Leland in 1546: 'The towne of Southton stondynge in a baren soyle fell dayly to decay, and the market was clene forsaken.' The Corporation of Sutton recorded in 1533 that it had been 'a poor ruinous country place . . . the inhabitants and working men both in and beyond the lordship [were] before completely destitute'. Perhaps these are slightly exaggerated accounts, contrasting the time before with the better times after the event, the event being the intervention of Bishop Vesey.

These near-contemporary accounts of Bishop Vesey's benefactions to Sutton show that he transformed the place on his own initiative. In order to achieve this, he needed wealth and power, and a concept of the reborn Sutton which he would create. He lived at a time when it was possible for someone of obscure origins to gain considerable wealth and power. He travelled in Europe and saw the flourishing cities on which his ideal Sutton might be modelled, and the new thinking of the Renaissance fuelled his desire to put his ideas into practice.

Bishop Vesey was the eldest son of a Sutton gentleman, William Harman, who had married Joan Squire, daughter of Henry Squire, Lord of the Manor of Handsworth. His supposed birthplace, a stone house in Moor Hall Drive, still stands, although this is more likely to be a house built in Vesey's lifetime on the site of his father's house. According to the inscription on his tomb in the parish church, he was born in 1452, but he is first heard of at Magdalen College, Oxford, in 1482. This throws doubt on the 1452 birth

The stone house in Moor Hall Drive, reputed birthplace of Bishop Vesey.

date, as it was usual to go to university before the age of twenty, so 1462 and 1465 have been suggested. However, his father had died in 1470, and if he was eighteen at the time he may have had family duties thrust upon him, or the family may have been in trouble over its Wars of the Roses allegiances, thus preventing him from going to Oxford until later.

At Oxford the new Renaissance scholarship was taking over from the medieval concentration on canon law, and the university was a vibrant and exciting place. Some

Rear view of the stone house, showing the tower that holds the spiral stair.

A Bishop Vesey Time Line

1452	Birth of John Harman alias Vesey
1470	Death of William Harman, Vesey's father; another son and two daughters had been born since John
1482	Entered Magdalen College, Oxford
1489	Joined the household of Elizabeth of York, Henry VII's queen
1494	Awarded the degree of Doctor of Laws by Oxford University
1495	Received the first of many Church preferments – Chaplain of the Free Chapel of St Blaise in Sutton Coldfield; at least fourteen more ecclesiastical offices were to be held by him
1509	Accession of Henry VIII
1508	Dean of Exeter
1514	Dean of the Chapel
1515	Became Registrar of the Order of the Garter. Read the Papal Bull at the investiture of Cardinal Wolsey
1516	Tutor to the infant Princess Mary, for whom a household was formed at Ludlow
1517	As a member of the King's Council (later known as the Star Chamber), he worked alongside Thomas More. Appointed Commissioner for enclosures in Berkshire and six other counties. Obtained the Chantry lands at Sutton Coldfield
1519	Bishop of Exeter
1520	Went to the Field of the Cloth of Gold with a retinue of 4 chaplains, 6 gentlemen, 23 servants and 20 horses. Was an executor of the will of the Earl of Derby
1522	Was one of the ecclesiastics who greeted the Emperor Charles V on his arrival at Dover
1523	His mother, Joan Harman, died at Sutton. Vesey went to Dover with the Earl of Devonshire to welcome the King of Denmark
1525	President of the Court of the Marches of Wales – effectively Governor of Wales, Gloucestershire, Herefordshire, Worcestershire, Salop and Cheshire
1527	He lived at Moor Hall, where he had 140 retainers in scarlet caps and gowns
1528	Sutton Coldfield Borough Charter. His brother-in-law, William Gibbons, was the first Warden (i.e. Mayor)
1529	His many benefactions
1530	His brother-in-law, John Leveson, was second Warden and Thomas Kene, his niece's husband, third Warden of Sutton
1532	Accompanied Henry VIII to Calais to visit Francis I of France
1534	Officiated at the consecration of Cranmer as Archbishop of Canterbury
1544	Sent 20 soldiers to the Battle of Boulogne
1549	Sent 40 men to assist the Earl of Warwick against Kett's Rebellion in Norfolk
1551	Resigned his See of Exeter
1553	Reinstated as Bishop of Exeter
1554	Death of Vesey

of Vesey's associates there held high office under Henry VII, while others, notably the future Cardinal Wolsey, would hold sway under Henry VIII. The Wars of the Roses had left the nobility discredited and exhausted, so men of merit from all backgrounds could rise in the new Tudor age.

In 1489 Vesey was appointed to a position in the household of Elizabeth, queen of Henry VII, where the future Henry VIII was born in 1491, and so began his diplomatic career, of which nothing is known except that it must have been lucrative. Officials were rewarded and promoted by receiving valuable Church appointments, and the list of these in Vesey's case is very long. When Henry VIII came to the throne in 1509, Vesey and Wolsey were two of his chief ministers. Both accompanied the new king on his royal progresses, Wolsey having the office of Almoner, and Vesey being Dean of the Chapel.

In 1515 Vesey officiated when Wolsey was created Cardinal, and in 1516 he was appointed tutor to the infant Princess Mary (the future Queen Mary I). In 1517 Sir Thomas More became a member of the King's Council, and it was Vesey who trained him in the busy schedule of settling legal disputes. More had recently written *Utopia*, a work depicting an ideal society, and was the friend of Erasmus of Rotterdam, the foremost scholar of the Renaissance. Perhaps their discussions included how to set up a model town. In 1519 Vesey became Bishop of Exeter, and in 1520 formed part of the glittering train attending Henry VIII to the Field of the Cloth of Gold.

In 1517 Vesey obtained the Chantry lands at Sutton after the dissolution of the Chantry, and he was in Sutton again when his mother died in 1523. After 1526 he seems to have played a smaller part on the national stage and in 1527 he acquired an estate to add to Moor Hall, which he had built a few years earlier, and where he lived in great style. He secured a charter to make Sutton a self-governing borough in 1528 and conferred great benefits on the town, including the grammar school of 1541 which bears his name. Some of the fifty-one stone houses he built can still be seen, but his attempt to establish the craft of kersey knitting (kerseys, a woollen cloth, was England's most valuable export in Tudor times) did not succeed.

Bishop Vesey died in 1554, aged 102 (or maybe only 89), having resigned the See of Exeter in 1551 under Edward VI, only to be reinstated in 1553 by Queen Mary. He seems to have enjoyed the favour of those Tudor monarchs that he had known in their childhood – perhaps he had been a father-figure to both Henry and Mary.

In 1533 the newly formed corporation of Sutton, the warden and society, showed its gratitude to Vesey by bestowing the lease of the town mill on Thomas Keene, who had married one of Vesey's nieces. The deed records:

Mindful of the many and great benefits conferred on us by the venerable father John Bishop of Exeter, who through his efforts, costs, works and expenses has

The original grammar school; painting by Paul Braddon based on an engraving in the Aylesford Collection.

caused the foresaid town of Sutton to change from a poor ruinous country place to one populous and flourishing, and the inhabitants and working men, both in and beyond the Lordship, before completely destitute, he has considerably enriched with houses and cattle, besides other benefits and gifts bestowed on us which we desire to mark with some gift.

A comprehensive list of these benefactions is given in Dugdale's *Antiquities of Warwickshire*, the principal one being the Borough Charter of 1528 which made Sutton a self-governing town. Although the king granted this, it was at Vesey's request. He built a town hall with a prison and covered market beneath, and paved the roads in the town. He built the school and endowed it, built the two aisles of the church and gave the organs, and built fifty-one stone houses, some of which are still standing. He stocked the park with mares, colts and horses, marking the boundary with a hedge and ditch, and enclosed the seven woods in Sutton Park. He disforested the chase

Stone house in Maney Hill Road, built by Bishop Vesey.

Stone house in Wylde Green Road, built by Bishop Vesey.

so that sheep could graze freely on the commons, and granted the coppices to the inhabitants as fuel. It was this large injection of capital, all aimed at improving the lot of the ordinary inhabitants of Sutton, which worked the transformation so obvious to contemporaries, but it was the Borough Charter that would have a more lasting effect.

The charter gave the government of Sutton to a corporation consisting of a warden and a society of twenty-four men. These men were to be chosen in 1529 by the

Bishop Vesey's tomb in Sutton Coldfield parish church.

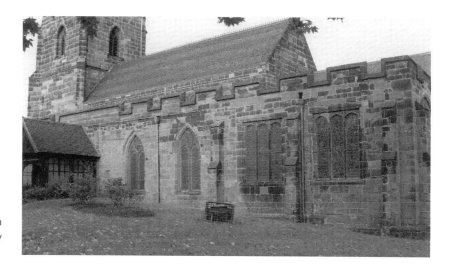

The south aisle of Sutton Coldfield parish church, built by Bishop Vesey.

inhabitants acting under the authority of the first warden, named in the charter as William Gibbons, one of Vesey's brothers-in-law. Thereafter any vacancies occurring were to be filled by men chosen by the rest of the society. The warden and society took over most of the authority and functions of the feudal lord. This included the collection of the income (assessed at £58) formerly accounted for by the bailiff. All the officers of the chase and park, who had been appointed by the Crown, continued to draw their salary for a time; when these offices were extinguished the full £58 was payable annually to the Crown by the warden and society. The courts continued as before, and the markets and fairs were reinstated. Some of the clauses reflect Vesey's expansionist plans, for example, the right of anyone to establish a farm on the waste lands, and others his concern for the well-being of all the inhabitants, such as the right of free warren (the freedom to hunt small game animals and birds) given to all the inhabitants.

The inscription on Vesey's tomb refers to him as a 'pious and learned prelate'. In a letter to his daughter, Sir Thomas More described him as 'a man of deep learning, and of a wide reputation for holiness'. Against the background of the ferment of ideas and new thinking associated with the Renaissance in England in the early years of the reign of Henry VIII, Vesey developed his ideas for creating a model town at Sutton Coldfield. He recognised that he would have to spend a great deal of money to set Sutton up as a prosperous town, but also that it needed institutions to allow it to develop into the flourishing Renaissance city he perhaps dreamed it might become. The foundation of the school and the granting of the charter provided the framework

The Borough Charter of 1528, now kept in the City of Birmingham Archives repository.

for the growth of a flourishing market town with a proliferation of trades. Anything more would depend on the drive and civic ambition of succeeding generations.

The sixteenth century in England was generally a period of economic growth and increasing population, and Sutton would eventually have recovered and flourished without the intervention of Bishop Vesey. He stands as a man of the Renaissance who created change, transforming Sutton from feudal stagnation to modern prosperity, but in some respects he was a man of his times. He was generous with his wealth to his family, securing good marriages for his nieces and giving them generous marriage settlements. The marriage settlement for his niece, Jane Harman, of 14 December 1525 survives; she was to marry George Middlemore of Haselwell (Stirchley). Bishop Vesey was party to the document. He gave £400 to George's father, who settled an income from his manor of Haselwell on Jane and declared that George would inherit it. The deeds were to be kept in a chest at Moor Hall under two locks, Vesey or his brother Hugh Harman to have one key, John Middlemore to have the other. Vesey was to hold the manor of Haselwell in trust with six of his nominees, all prominent gentry in the Sutton area, showing the local following he could command. A medieval touch is the proviso that if Jane should die before the wedding, George would marry one of her sisters, and another is the proviso that John Middlemore could leave money to secure annual prayers for himself in Kings Norton church and Moseley chapel after his death; the Church was still in an unreformed state in 1525.

SIX

Sutton Coldfield the Market Town, 1528-1824

Population

At the beginning of the sixteenth century the population of Sutton was probably between 500 and 600, no higher than it had been in 1400. There would have been about 40 houses in Great Sutton, 40 in Hill and Little Sutton, and 20 in each of the other three quarters, Maney and the Wild, Walmley and Beyond the Wood, and More and Ashfurlong. It is possible to name most of the householders from 1546, when a series of court rolls for Sutton begins, and a good proportion of them are mentioned in one capacity or another. Some of the court rolls record that households were sheltering 'inmakes', newcomers to the area, the general growth of population having produced an increase in vagrancy and displaced people. From 1565 the parish register records the baptisms, marriages and burials, giving a more comprehensive list of names. Using these sources it is possible to deduce that the population of Sutton was growing throughout the sixteenth century roughly in proportion to the growth in the national population. By 1600 it had doubled to approximately 1,000 (the population of England rose from about 2,200,000 in 1500 to 4,100,000 in 1600).

The growth of population continued in the seventeenth century, as can be seen from the parish register. In the years 1614 to 1619 there were 190 baptisms, whereas there were only 158 burials from 1620 to 1624 (32 more births than deaths). From 1685 to 1690 there were 259 baptisms, but in the following five-year period, from 1691 to 1695, only 187 burials, 72 more births than deaths. Infant mortality was high for both

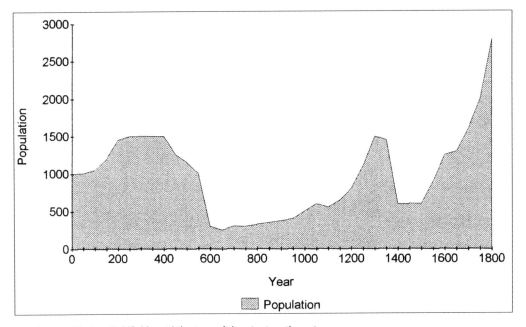

Population of Sutton Coldfield, until the turn of the nineteenth century.

1620–4 and 1691–5. One in three burials was of a child, and only 75 per cent of the children born survived infancy. The simple growth of population by excess of births over deaths is complicated by other factors, notably migration. Bishop Vesey had deliberately encouraged new people to come and settle in Sutton by building houses, stocking the park and including a clause in the charter to encourage colonisation of the commons. He tried to establish the craft of kersey knitting in the town by importing craftsmen from Honeybourne in Worcestershire; some of them stayed although their craft died out in Sutton.

Migration is reflected in the parish register by the disappearance of surnames as families die out or move away, and by the introduction of new surnames not previously recorded. This can be illustrated from the marriage register for 1655, where unusual detail is given for thirteen marriages. In January Thomas Stafford, a cooper, married Elizabeth Croxall, both of Sutton Coldfield, but neither of them was born in the town. Likewise in May John Wood and Ann Bach of Sutton were married, but neither appears in the baptismal register. In June Edward Greensill, a nailer of Sutton who was born in Water Orton, married Elizabeth Hunniburne, born here in 1633, and John Hopkins of Sutton, born in Erdington, married Ann Hadley of Halesowen. In August John Foxxe, a nailer born in Sutton in 1624, married Ann Wilkason, a widow of the town, while in

September Mr George Sand from Shropshire married Brigett Swynfen, daughter of Mr Richard Swynfen Esq. of Sutton. There are a further seven entries for 1655 but some of them record the banns of marriages that took place elsewhere. Five of these twenty-six people were not from Sutton, two had already settled here from elsewhere, and only eight had been born in Sutton; details of the other eleven are not given.

The marriage register for 1655 throws light on the make-up of the population of Sutton. At this time the titles *Mr* and *Mrs* specifically identified gentry. In the rigid social structure of the time the gentry comprised the upper stratum of society, whose income was derived from property or other sources; a gentleman 'never worked with his hands on necessary, as opposed to leisurely, activities'. Next in line were the yeomen, substantial farmers renting their farms and perhaps owning some land, and they were followed by the husbandmen who were lesser farmers with no land of their own. Labourers and paupers made up the lowest level. Of the thirteen marriages of 1655, two were gentry, none were yeomen (although there were several in the next two years), two were husbandmen, six were tradesmen and the other three were not described. The tradesmen included a cooper, a chandler, a stirrup-maker and three nailers.

The tradesmen fitted into the structure of society according to the nature and scale of their trade. A poor nailer might be in the bottom layer of society, while a substantial chandler would be the equivalent of a yeoman. Other sources can be used to find out more about occupations. There are some surviving wills and inventories of property, but not everyone made a will, and a more comprehensive listing is found in the Hearth Tax records. These records were made to show who had paid their hearth tax in the 1670s, and should list every householder. The lists show that 12 per cent of the householders were gentry compared with the 5–10 per cent for most of the parishes in England. Conversely, the number of pauper households is also large, between 31 and 41 per cent compared with a national average of 30 per cent. Paupers were those in receipt of parish relief, so the number varied from year to year as circumstances changed. Parish relief was administered by the churchwardens, and was a successor to the alms given by the tithingmen in the fifteenth century. Sutton was attractive to gentry as it was a congenial place with some good houses with modest estates and excellent hunting, while the extensive commons gave opportunities to poor squatters to gain a foothold. Of the ninety-eight houses receiving relief in 1670, thirty were 'upon the common'.

The Hearth Tax records also give an idea of the distribution of the population, with two of the quarters, Maney and Wild, and Warmley and Beyond the Woods,

Part of the Hearth Tax record for 'Hill Quarter and Little Sutton', 1673 (now in Warwick Record Office). The entries in the right-hand column indicate forges; these were exempt from the tax because they were used in connection with a trade.

each having 47 households, 13 of them poor. There were 46 houses in Moore and Ashfurlong, 9 of them belonging to gentry, but this quarter had poor areas as well as big houses, with 19 households in receipt of relief. Hill and Little Sutton was a much more populous quarter, with 101 houses. The list separates Hill from Little Sutton: Hill has 37 paupers, many of them no doubt in Hill Hook, Four Oaks and the cottages near Watford Gap, while Little Sutton has only 11; there are only 5 gentry altogether. It is in the town (Great Sutton) that we find the most gentry households with 13, most of them no doubt occupying the substantial houses along High Street and Coleshill Street. The pauper households mostly lived in cottages at the bottom of the hill, and numbered 33 out of a total of 77 houses in Great Sutton.

In 1674, according to the Hearth Tax, there were 314 houses and the total population was about 1,400. The steady growth in numbers continued and was recorded by successive rectors. In 1698 there were said to be 322 houses, listed by quarter in roughly the same proportions as in the Hearth Tax, except that Hill had grown from 64 to 70 houses, of which 28 were at Hill Hook. Walmley, with only 19 houses, was also given separately. In 1721 there were 360 houses, of which 107 were in Great Sutton, a growth of 29 houses since 1698. Most of these must have been substantial houses, as only 19 cottages are specified. The other area of growth was More and Ashfurlong, where most of the additional 12 houses were cottages, probably many of them on Reddicap Heath – there were 29 cottages altogether in this quarter. Walmley suffered a slight decline; only 18 houses were there, but no cottages. In 1762 the population was estimated at 1,800, and in 1772 the Revd R.B. Riland said 376 households received communion at Easter. This figure should have been comprehensive, as everyone was expected to do their Easter duty, but the figure seems low compared with the 504 households estimated in 1784. The rector then noted that there were 485 houses, 19 of which contained two households, and 53 of them were freehold. There were 106 cottages, a high figure, but less than the 116 recorded in 1721, so perhaps the town was now more prosperous. He gave the total population as 2,487, of which 1,126 were children. This high proportion of children, nearly half the population, reflects the relatively low life expectancy at the time, which has been estimated at 35 years. The rector was probably right in saying that people were migrating away from Sutton, no doubt heading to the fast-growing towns of the time. The rest of the population is given as: 166 single women, 808 married people and 387 servants and inmates. These figures appear to show that the population grew by over 50 per cent between 1762 and 1784. Such a high rate of growth is very unlikely, and it seems the estimate for 1762 is probably too low. In 1801 an accurate figure, 2,847, was given by the first official census; the figure for 1821 was 3,450.

Agriculture and Economy

At the time of the charter of 1528 Sutton was primarily an agricultural area, with most of the farmland contained within field systems and each farmer having a number of strips in these fields. The heavy plough drawn by a team of oxen was still the normal implement of cultivation, and there are a few places in Sutton where the ridges and furrows formed by the medieval plough can still be seen. Sometimes the field boundaries are slightly curved, forming a very shallow reversed 'S' shape, known as the aratral curve; this was made by the course of the plough as it approached the headland where it would be turned (see page 29). In his will of 1671, John Greasebrook mentions, among the land he is bequeathing, 'a way or convenient passage to turn a team'. The Tudor court rolls for Sutton laid down orders for the management of the open fields, particularly regarding the maintenance of the stock-proof hedges or fences round the open fields, with every farmer being responsible for his own section.

In 1567 a survey was made of a farm in Little Sutton belonging to John Chattocke and leased to William Croxall. It is only 19 acres, little more than a subsistence farm, but the land is listed in fourteen different units, for example 'two lands lying together in Shadwell Field'. In all there are thirty-seven 'lands' or strips, probably approximately 11 yards by 220 yards. The strips are distributed through the three open fields of Little Sutton, and each is described as lying between the strips belonging to other tenants – eighteen different tenants are named as having neighbouring strips. The three fields, each about 80 acres, probably supported about sixteen farms of a similar size, a way of farming which had changed little for over 500 years. As well as the arable land Croxall's farm included some of the meadow which lay next to the 'water gutter' (now covered by the houses at the Little Sutton Lane end of Heathcroft Road), providing the necessary winter fodder for his draught animals.

Among the probate records in the Diocesan Record Office at Lichfield is the will and inventory of John Greasebrook the elder of Wigginshill, yeoman, who died at the end of May 1671. He bequeathed his land to his three grandsons, and gave detailed descriptions of twenty separate units of land, which included twenty-three lands or

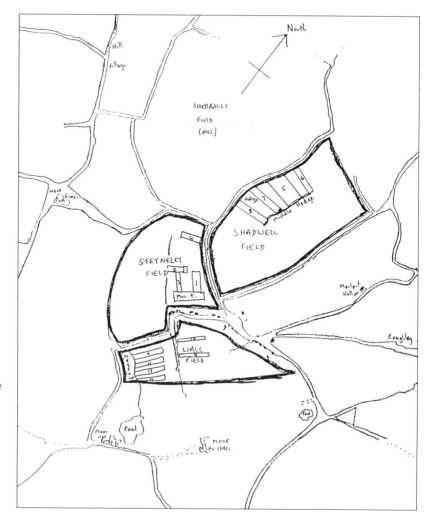

Plan to show the distribution of the 'lands' of William Croxall's farm in the open fields of Little Sutton in 1567. To the south of Wall Field is the Moor Hall Estate.

ridges in the three common fields pertaining to the twin hamlets of Wigginshill and Greaves, named as Church Field, Greaves Field and Wigginshill Field. He details the heads and baulks belonging to these ridges (that is, the ends where the plough was turned). He also had 2 or 3 acres of meadow in the common meadows named Broad Meadow and Orton Meadow, bounded on one side by the River Tame. Most of John Greasebrook's wealth, as listed in the inventory, was in the value of his agricultural goods – these were valued at £118 compared with £25 for the goods in the house. The inventory lists the growing crops – 11 days' work of wheat, 1½ days' work of blencorn (wheat and rye together), 11 days' work of peas, 2 acres of barley, 1 acre of oats and some hemp (for making rope and coarse cloth). This is about equal proportions of

Little Sutton open fields superimposed on a modern map.

autumn-sown and spring-sown crops, suggesting that the age-old three-year rotation was still being observed (a day's work was sometimes used interchangeably with an acre as a measure of growing crops). Stored in the house were eleven strikes of blencorn and a strike of wheat from the previous year's harvest (a strike was a measure of volume, normally 4 bushels or 32 gallons) and six strikes of malt.

Also stored in the house of John Greasebrook were eighteen cheeses, an indication that it was a mixed farm. More than half the value of his agricultural goods was accounted for by livestock, including 34 sheep and 12 cows in addition to the oxen and horses. In his will, the land detailed includes six closes and some pasture ground. These closes would be the smaller square fields with stock-proof hedges which were gradually supplanting the old open fields as the normal pattern of farming. The smaller fields gave the farmer the flexibility to convert from arable to pasture and back, and allowed him to take advantage of the new methods of agriculture being introduced. This process of change from common fields to the smaller square units was very slow in Wigginshill, where open fields and strips were still marked on a map of 1825. There are only one or two strips surviving from the old fields of Hill and Little Sutton on the 1824 map, and none in Maney or Great Sutton. Although all the land detailed in the survey of William Croxall's farm at Little Sutton in 1569 consisted of strips in the common fields, some of his neighbours had already made their land into closes with their own fences or hedges round them, the bounds of some of Croxall's strips being described as 'several', that is enclosed with a fence (see the map on page 63, where the plot labelled 'Mrs Y.' in Steyneley Field is described as 'several' land belonging to Mrs Yardley). This long process of turning the open or common fields into the familiar patchwork of smaller, squarer fields seems to have been achieved by local agreement, leaving no direct records. Perhaps some of the fines handed out at the courts in Elizabethan times for breaking and burning of fences and hedges show that the process was not always welcomed.

In 1762 an article on Sutton appeared in *The Gentleman's Magazine*, in which the writer described the local farming practice:

The method of tillage is usually to plough up the turf in the spring, after which the land lies fallow during the summer, and at Michelmas [25 September] a crop of wheat is sown, after which three more crops are taken successively of barley, oats or peas; with the last of these crops is sown clover, or rye-grass, to bring a turf again, which must continue for six or even ten years before it is broken up again, otherwise the land will be too much impoverished.

Pond in a field near Bulls Lane, formed by the extraction of marl to spread on the land.

This is not unlike the classic Norfolk four-course rotation (turnips – clover – wheat – barley) of the Agricultural Revolution. A similar article was published locally at the same time, together with a response from another writer calling himself 'Agricola', who disagreed with most of the statements in the original:

> Turnips and Barley are the most profitable produce of our lands, which if in good power, will also afford a subsequent crop of wheat or peas; and after that one crop (only) of spring corn with seeds . . . it is the practice of one of the most experienced judges in this neighbourhood to have his land two years up and two years down; that is, two years in tillage, and two in clover.

Generally the soil in Sutton was light and sandy, and a common method of improving its texture was to spread marl (clay) over the surface. It was easy to find pockets of marl in most parts of Sutton. The extraction of marl created a pit which subsequently filled with water, and almost every field had its duck pond or 'marl pit' as a result of this process.

Sometimes the method of cultivation is specified in the terms of a lease. A lease dated 13 June 1828 for seven years of three fields in Maney, including a field of about seven acres called Stoney Leasow (the site now occupied by Sutton Coldfield Grammar School for Girls), lays down such conditions. One half of Stoney Leasow was to be manured and sown with turnips, then sheep were to eat off the turnips; it was to be sown with barley the following year, then clover and rye grass for pasture for two years. The other half of Stoney Leasow was to be limed, then sown with wheat, then clover and rye grass for pasture. After each crop either 2½ tons of lime or 5 tons of manure was to be applied.

The management of the meadow land had also been improved by adopting a system of flooding the meadows in the winter months using timber barriers with simple sluice gates. The deposition of silt improved the fertility of the meadow, pests and diseases were controlled, and a better crop of hay could be taken earlier in the year. This process, known as 'floating', is documented in the New Hall Valley and at Eachelhurst, and wooden remains observed near New Hall in 1999 were probably part of a system for floating the meadows there. By 1820 most of the agricultural land in Sutton was being intensively managed in small fields by farmers who took advantage of advances in farming practice, alternating their land between arable and pasture.

In 1528 yeomen, husbandmen and agricultural labourers made up the bulk of the population of Sutton, all deriving their living from the land. But there were also tradesmen, and the commercial and craft industry side of the Sutton economy was on the increase. The Elizabethan court rolls mention the miller, the bakers, innkeepers and ale-sellers, a tailor and a shoemaker, and there are a few cases of fines for people tanning leather or processing parchment. Reference has already been made to the marriages register for 1655, where six of the thirteen bridegrooms were tradesmen (a cooper, a chandler, a stirrup-maker and three nailers). This was exceptional, as the twenty-one marriages in 1654 and 1656 involved only three tradesmen (a carpenter, a cooper and a tailor) compared with twelve husbandmen and three yeomen. In the few years for which the register gives this information, husbandman and nailer are the commonest descriptions.

The probate records for Sutton from 1665 to 1700 also show a high proportion of tradesmen. There are 129 probate records arising from the deaths of people in Sutton over this period, 21 of which relate to gentry and 32 give no description. Of the remaining 76, 23 are tradesmen. Thomas Clifton, a dyer and shearman, lived next to the Three Tuns in High Street, and the probate inventory refers to a workshop containing his dyeing equipment and a shop with shears, cutting boards, a shear board and 20 yards of woollen new cloth. Outside were the 'tenters' where the dyed cloth could be stretched out to dry. The value of his inventory is £65, showing that he was moderately prosperous, but more than half of his wealth was due to the value of his livestock and farm crops. Like most of the other tradesmen, he was also a part-time farmer with a few fields to cultivate. This makes analysis difficult, as some of the husbandmen may have been part-time nailers, for example, eking out their farming

High Heath Farm Cottage before renovation. A survey of 1811 lists two households living here, headed by William Taylor and George Oreton; it was then known as Swash Vale or Swarfs Dale.

The gable end of the half of High Heath Farm Cottage once occupied by George Oreton. The survey of 1811 refers to a weaving shop (i.e. workshop) here. Such workshops were often provided with a 'weaver's window', like the large window in the upper storey.

with a trade just as the tradesmen supplemented their income by farming. There are 129 probate records but 314 houses, so less than half the households are represented, and those are mostly the wealthier ones with something worth bequeathing. There were many like John Phillips the tailor, whose goods were worth only £8.

Three of the twenty-three tradesmen with probate records were millers. In 1528 there was only the manor mill at the bottom of Mill Street, which had the monopoly of grinding all the grain grown in Sutton. This monopoly was still in force in 1549 when the court roll contains the following order: 'And it is ordered that no person having a mill outside this lordship carry any grain or malt out of this lordship to be milled there unless it is his own grain or malt on pain of 6s 8d for each offence.' But the monopoly seems to have been broken by 1570, and at the end of Elizabeth's reign there was a fulling mill at Bracebridge, a blade mill at Park House, a corn mill at New Hall, corn, fulling and blade mills at Penns, a corn mill at Langley Mill, probably a corn mill at Hill Hook, and possibly a mill for sawing timber at Wyndley. These were all speculative ventures set up for commercial gain by men with capital to invest, and not all of them succeeded. Fulling ceased in Sutton early in the seventeenth century, and the blade mill at Park House had been demolished by 1650. However, the blade mill was re-established early in the eighteenth century, and mills with their attendant pools were built at Blackroot, Powells and Longmoor in the 1700s. The old manor mills had ceased to grind corn but were used instead for processing leather, while gunbarrels were bored at Holland House. According to *The Gentleman's Magazine* in 1762:

Some rivulets that take their rise in this park feed several mills built in and near it, not only for grinding corn, but for boring musket-barrels, polishing metal buttons, making saws, grinding axes, knives, bayonets, and performing various other operations for the mechanical traders in Birmingham.

Some of the mills were busy enough to employ several skilled workmen, and supported a number of the cottage industries which flourished in the eighteenth century. Nail-making, blacksmithing and making harness fittings for the saddle-makers of Walsall all involved metalwork, so by 1800 Sutton seemed set to join its neighbours in south Staffordshire in becoming a smoky industrial town. The corn mills were also thriving; successive leases of New Hall Mill show that it was common for a corn factor or a master baker to lease the mill and install a miller to work for him. Improvements

New Hall Mill.

The milling floor inside New Hall Mill.

in the design and strength of mill machinery made the mill more productive as the eighteenth century progressed and the surviving watermill building at New Hall Mill, dating from about 1780, housed four pairs of millstones.

Local Politics and Religion

The charter of 1528 provided for the establishment of a corporation consisting of a warden and a society made up of 24 members. The first warden, William Gibbons, was appointed, but the society was chosen by the householders of Sutton from among their number. At the time there were fewer than 200 households – so each member could be said to represent about eight households, a very democratic arrangement. Once established, the society maintained itself by choosing new members whenever existing members died or went away, and so it tended to become an exclusive group regarded with suspicion by non-members. Few records of the activities of the corporation survive before 1727 when the series of minutes of their meetings begins.

The gentry families residing in Sutton would mostly have been literate and articulate enough for politics to be aired and national events to be discussed. Early in the seventeenth century there were several rectors with puritan leanings, and the less authoritarian doctrines they preached seem to have found favour in Sutton. When civil war broke out in 1641 Sutton was predominantly Parliamentarian and, along with the rest of Warwickshire, was held for the parliamentary side throughout the war, returning Puritans to the Interregnum parliaments. The rector, Antony Burgess,

Vesey House.

Rear view of Vesey House, originally a courtyard house with stone-mullioned windows.

became a chaplain in Cromwell's New Model Army, while Thomas Willoughby took a more active role. His father had been warden of Sutton in 1626, he was related to the Willoughbys of Middleton and he lived at Vesey House in High Street. Early in the war he commanded a detachment of foot soldiers (probably including some Sutton men) who distinguished themselves at the Battle of Hopton Heath in Stafford by standing firm when most of the army was running away. He was an active member of the committee which administered Warwickshire for the Parliament, and was a county magistrate; he became a Member of Parliament in 1656. He died in 1661 and his friend Anthony Burgess would have erected a handsome memorial to him in the parish church had he not been ejected for non-conformity before it was ready. The political mood in Sutton then swung to the right, with Jacobite sympathies predominant by the end of the century.

A census was made in 1676 of those taking communion at Easter, and it gives figures for Sutton of 500 Anglicans, 40 Nonconformists and three Papists. In 1672 the Nonconformists had a licensed meeting-house at the home of Samuel Stevenson in High Street (possibly now no. 36). Stevenson was active in county politics and was made Sheriff of Warwickshire in 1697. He probably supported the Glorious Revolution, the Protestant Succession and the supremacy of Parliament. He was made a county magistrate in 1690, along with many other Whig gentlemen of the county, replacing the high Tories and Catholics who had been appointed in the reigns of Charles II and James II in their attempts to subdue Parliament. The Independent group originally met at his house, later became Baptists and had a chapel by 1800 on the site later occupied by the Catholic church, now known as the Guild Hall. There was a Quaker meeting-house in Wigginshill

The Quaker meeting-house at Wigginshill, now converted into a private house.

in 1686. The Sutton and Wishaw Quaker meetings combined with the Wigginshill meeting to buy a cottage, garden and orchard at Wigginshill in 1711, where a meeting-house was built in 1724. In the late eighteenth century it was fashionable for Birmingham Quaker couples to be married at Wigginshill, but the meeting-house closed down in 1830. Another Independent chapel was established in a room in a cottage in Roughley near Little Sutton in 1770 by the followers of a local gentleman, Abraham Austin, who later became a prominent figure in the Baptist church in the Birmingham area.

Meanwhile the High church interest was also active. George Sacheverell of New Hall in Sutton was made Sheriff of Derbyshire in 1709 (he owned property there),

The Baptist chapel at Little Sutton.

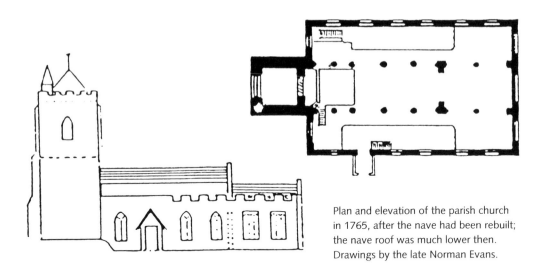

Plan and elevation of the parish church in 1765, after the nave had been rebuilt; the nave roof was much lower then. Drawings by the late Norman Evans.

Sketch by Miss Bracken, showing the church before the nave roof was raised. (*Norman Evans Collection*)

and he appointed his distant relative Henry Sacheverell to be his chaplain. Both were ardent Jacobites, but the sermons preached by Henry Sacheverell upset the Whigs, especially Henry Chadwick the deputy sheriff, and Henry Sacheverell was arraigned for treason. He was found guilty but not sentenced, an outcome regarded by local Tories as a triumph. He preached at Sutton church on 20 October 1714 to a congregation that included 200 Birmingham Jacobites, and the result was a riot. In 1715 Chadwick inherited New Hall on the death of his uncle George Sacheverell, and Henry departed. By 1762 Sutton was 'an agreeable neighbourhood; which last circumstance is chiefly owing to a total extinction of party-zeal, a mischievous passion which raged here with all its baleful influence about ten or twelve years ago'.

The parish church, meanwhile, was in poor condition and in 1760 a programme of rebuilding began, using 'a sort of hard sandstone, of which there is a plentiful quarry within the distance of half a mile'. When the rebuilding was complete, controversy arose over the pews. Most of the substantial houses in Sutton carried a right to the use of a particular pew in the parish church. When the pews in the rebuilt church were allocated, many dissatisfied owners claimed that they had been fobbed off with pews obscured by new pillars, or further away from the pulpit. The situation was exacerbated by the knowledge that public money had been used to finance the rebuilding, and some of the resentment was directed at the warden and society. The society had considerable income from the land and property it owned, which was to be used for the good of the inhabitants, but when a capital sum was needed it was raised by the sale of timber. In 1762 there was more than £5,000-worth of wood growing in Sutton Park – a ready source of capital. Good woodland management dictated that a certain amount of felling should be done from time to time in any case. However, because the society had become an exclusive body, non-members were inclined to suspect corruption every time a substantial amount of timber was sold.

The warden and society joined the townsfolk in 1778 in opposing a plan to enclose the commons. On 22 April 1778 a meeting of over 150 inhabitants at the Three Tuns Inn had declared its unanimous opposition, but distrust of the corporation lingered on. In 1788 a complaint against the corporation was laid in the Court of Chancery by William Twamley and others, alleging that timber had been sold below its true value and that corporation land had been enclosed and leased at inadequate rents. The Court of Chancery required the warden and society to seek the approval of one of its Masters before taking any innovative action, and this effectively tied the hands of the corporation for the next thirty-six years. For instance, early in the nineteenth century Mr Perkins

Above, left: The Old Smithy at Maney, a timber-framed house of cruck construction.
Above, right: A stone house at Wylde Green Road, showing the massive chimney.
Below: Timber-framed house at Wigginshill with stone footings.

Plan showing the location of the old grammar school. The base map is the Corporation Survey of 1811. Marked on the plan at (1) is the site of the grammar school; according to the warden and society minutes, the workhouse was subsequently built on this site. Marked (2) is the site of the schoolmaster's house, shown on Snape's map of 1767; this may have been the original St Mary's Hall, a medieval building which became part of the school property. Marked (3) is the schoolmaster's garden, later added to the churchyard. These school properties were near the top of the hill and looked out over a jumble of sixteen cottages with their outbuildings and gardens.

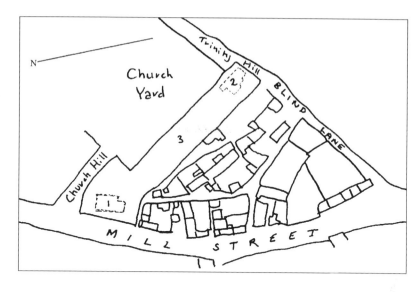

applied to renew his lease of Blackroot Pool for twenty-one years, but the corporation minutes for 12 March 1802 record 'we conceive ourselves restrained by an Injunction from the Court of Chancery from granting such renewal', and they could only offer a renewal from year to year.

Housing, Education, Social Life and the Arts

Bishop Vesey built fifty-one stone houses for the inhabitants of Sutton between 1525 and 1535, but his own house, Moor Hall, was built of brick, as were the great Tudor palaces of Greenwich, Nonsuch and Hampton Court. The usual building materials in Sutton had been timber for the frame, wattle and daub for the walls, and thatch for the roof. Before 1500 most houses were of one storey and had no chimney, the smoke from the open hearth escaping through vents in the thatch. All the Vesey houses had both chimneys and upper storeys, and by the end of Elizabeth's reign there were hardly any houses in Sutton without these features, although the half-timbered style continued to be preferred. The grammar school founded by Bishop Vesey for the education of the boys of the parish was also built of stone and stood not far from the church at the top of Mill Street. The trustees of the school were accused of malpractice before long, and new trustees were appointed on better terms. The school thrived or languished according to the qualities of the headmaster. It did not meet all the needs of the parish and other schools were set up from time to time; the parish register records the death in 1690 of Mr Barton, schoolmaster, of Hill.

John Elly, headmaster of Bishop Vesey's School, died in 1659, and the inventory of his goods and chattels includes the item 'tables, desks, pales and writings belonging to the school', valued at £10. The thirteen stools and chairs and two tables in the parlour, presumably of better quality than the school furniture, were worth about 25s, so there must have been places for over thirty day pupils. Elly also had a large collection of books, valued at £8 (not many inventories mention books, but Henry Mott, gentleman, who died in 1662, had books worth 13s), a viol and a cittern (a kind of lute). John Elly's inventory also gives us an idea of the layout of his living accommodation, as the items are valued room by room. Apart from the old kitchen and the new kitchen, the only ground-floor room mentioned is the parlour, so perhaps the rest of the ground floor was taken up with the school. Upstairs there was a chamber over the parlour, a matted chamber, a middle chamber and a little long-chamber, and on the second floor a chamber over the middle chamber. Also mentioned is a 'bay of stone building', which was probably an extension. (A 'bay of building' was the full width of the building between two structural cross-pieces known as trusses.)

Most of the timber-framed buildings in Sutton were two, three or four-bay houses. In 1692 the inventory of William Pickerell refers to a room called the 'house', which was probably two bays of the ground floor separated from the third bay (the parlour) by a screened passage running from the front door to the back door. The chambers

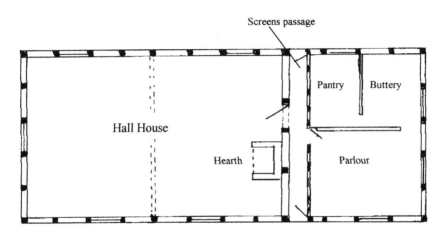

Plan of a typical three-bay house.

over the parlour and over the house were both bedrooms, while the 'cheese chamber', probably at the far end, was a small store-room. Although Pickerell was a moderately prosperous yeoman, his house was sparsely furnished, with none of the comforts of John Elly, who had feather-beds, curtains, carpets and rugs, hangings and court cupboards. Elly had pewter and brass worth £4, while Pickerell had eighteen wooden trenchers worth a penny each.

Throughout the seventeenth century there was a strong motivation to learn to read, particularly among the Puritans, since salvation seemed to depend on being able to read the revealed truths of the Bible. But under John Elly the pupils would have come into contact with music, books and culture to give them a fuller education. In 1683 a petition was drawn up for the householders of Sutton to sign. It contains 145 names; 78 of the names are marked by the petitioner with a cross and the name written beside it by someone else, but 67 are signed. The ability to sign one's name shows a level of education and indicates literacy in most cases, while inability to write does not necessarily mean inability to read, so perhaps 50 per cent of this sample were literate.

The old grammar school was in a poor state in 1727, and a new school house was built in 1728, now part of the present Bishop Vesey's Grammar School. The corporation contributed to the cost of this, in return for the headmaster, Paul Lowe, agreeing to teach twelve parish boys writing, arithmetic and English. One such parish boy was Zachariah Twamley, who later wrote:

Bishop Vesey's Grammar School, Lichfield Road, showing the 1728 building.

In the month of January 1780 after the Christmas holidays of 1779 were ended and the school reopened again; my next older brother Samuel with myself we were both admitted by the Head Master into the school; in the English department of the said school. It now last January 1855 was seventy-five years ago. I was then aged 7 years and 5 months. Having been taught to read, which at that time was the qualification required for admission, I was first placed in the reading class, amongst about a dozen more boys and continued in the same class for some months afterwards, all the time free from any weekly payments.

After a year Twamley had to pay 6*d* a week to be taught spelling, reading, writing and arithmetic by the under-master. William Webb was the headmaster at this time but after his death no more parish boys were taught there.

When the new grammar school was built in 1728, that part of Lichfield Road was considered a suitable site for high-status houses. Moat House had been built by the architect

Moat House.

Sir William Wilson before 1700, and on the opposite side of the road were The Anchorage and The Rookery, both dating from about 1750. The Rookery, built for the Jessons of Langley Hall, was said to be the finest example of Georgian architecture in Sutton: 'The greatest ornament and addition to the buildings in the town of Sutton, is the house of William Jesson Esq. (most remarkable for its neatness of situation).' Many of the houses in High Street belonged to leading local families, but the old stone or timber-framed buildings did not suit the taste of the time:

Right: Bust of Jane Pudsey on the Pudsey Memorial by William Wilson in Sutton parish church.

Below: Moat House, drawn by Snape in about 1760, showing the row of urns that once adorned the balustrade.

Bottom: Rear of Moat House, showing some original windows with mullions and transoms.

No. 38 High Street, with a façade of five sash windows, the centre one being a dummy window painted on the brick wall for effect.

No. 1 High Street – 'an elegant single-plane brick façade, filled with symmetrically arranged sash windows'.

Below: No. 46 High Street.
Below, right: A pilastered and pedimented doorcase in High Street.

Timber-framing at the rear of 36 High Street.

Stone construction at the rear of 38 High Street.

No. 1 High Street, showing the join between the brick front and the stone gable.

Proportion and symmetry were the underlying principles of the new architectural language . . . the front might simply be ripped off and replaced with an elegant single-plane brick façade, filled with symmetrically arranged sash windows, and adorned with some tasteful classical ornament, such as a pilastered and pedimented doorcase.

Most of the inhabitants of Sutton worked long hours on the land, but even so they found plenty of opportunities for socialising. There were formal occasions, like church on Sunday and the twice-yearly courts, while the two annual fairs and the weekly Monday markets were more informal. At a court held in 1558 three innkeepers and five ale-sellers were fined. Another court threatened all victuallers that if they failed to comply with a court order, then they must cease trading and take down their inn signs. Some of the social gatherings were evidently not very convivial, as fights and brawls were reported at every court. Often the fine was 4*d*, giving rise to the phrase 'give him a fourpenny one', which is still sometimes to be heard. In 1547 the court fined three innkeepers 6*d* for 'allowing servants to play illicit games in their houses at the time of divine service', and in 1559 it was ordered 'that if anyone allows other people to play at bowls in their gardens or plecks he shall forfeit 6*s* 8*d* for each offence'.

The two annual fairs were big occasions, each lasting three days. The Trinity Fair was held in June while the October fair took place on the feast of St Simon and St Jude (28 October). The Tudor courts ordered the archery butts to be set up in advance of the Trinity Fair, everyone being required to be able to handle a longbow in Elizabethan times, and the constable was ordered to see that the fairs were properly policed. Horse-traders came to the fair, paying a market fee or toll on every transaction. The toll book for 1750–1 survives, recording seven horses bought on 11 June 1750, fourteen on 28 October and twenty-one and nineteen respectively at the next two fairs in 1751. The traders mostly came from towns in neighbouring counties such as Hinckley, Stone and Stourbridge, but some came from as far away as Lincolnshire and Shropshire.

In 1554 the court ordered all the inhabitants of the town to clean their street frontages 'before the feast of Simon and Jude', and 300 years later the bustle of the fair was still occupying the frontages:

Early in the morning on a Fair day people came and tied hurdles all along the footpaths to make sheep pens. There are still staples in the barn wall which were used for that purpose. [This barn was at nos 1, 3 and 5 Coleshill Street,

The Old Rectory, nos 1, 3 and 5 Coleshill Street.

Rear of the Old Rectory, showing the stone construction of the main range.

Sharpening stones under the archway at the Old Rectory.

The Old Top Swan, Lichfield Road. (*Norman Evans Collection*)

The Golden Cup in Birmingham Road, drawn by K.J. Williams.

which had been the Rectory in the seventeenth century; under the archway are some stones with marks made by the sharpening of arrowheads (see page 85).] Sutton was 'en fête' in those days. Cattle and sheep and pigs hustled about and horses trotted up and down in the hollow. Booths occupied the middle of the town hall . . . in the stalls was yellow rock, ginger bread, brandy soup and nuts, in the booths teefee caffirs . . . and all sorts of wild animals.

There were shooting galleries and freak shows, and the crowds poured in from all directions. 'If you desired to see real pomp you should have seen the fair proclaimed. The Sergeant at Mace and certain old crippled friends with halberds, and the crier, undertook this responsible duty.'

Bonfire night was another occasion for celebration, as was the annual inauguration of the new warden on 2 November. In 1747 the blacksmith, Thomas Standley, was at a parish meeting to celebrate this event ('Warduins Choice') with many friends at the Red Lion. At ten o'clock at night he went out to relieve himself and drowned in a well.

By the eighteenth century the inns and public houses had begun to adopt their now-familiar names. There was a case in 1769 of someone passing counterfeit money, but when the constable arrived at the Horse and Jockey the suspect was not there, so he next called in at the Golden Cup and found a man offering to sell shillings for sixpence. There are references to the Barley Mow and the White Lion in Hill, and the Talbot, later known as the Dog, at the foot of Mill Street. In Sutton there had been a Woolpack and a Bear, and there are references to the Three Tuns and the Red Lion. In Little Sutton there was the Fox and Dogs.

These last three inns are named in the Coroner's Papers, as some of the inquests were held there. Some Coroner's Papers survive for the period 1740–70. Although they deal primarily with tragic events, the papers also include the direct testimony of people who were going about their everyday business at the time of the death. We hear of a boy, John Gorton, going on an errand in Wylde Green in January 1762 and stopping to play at 'gliding' on a frozen pond with another boy; of three 14-year-olds playing on the green at Little Sutton in 1751, one of whom picked up a gun in the blacksmith's shop which accidentally went off. In November 1762 William Jesson's servant was out with his master's hounds near Rectory Park hunting hares with a friend, William Allport, when the latter fell from his horse and was killed. These cameos show us the quiet routine life of a country market town. There always seemed to be someone within call – when a farmworker went for a swim after work and drowned in a pond, he was immediately missed, and in 1740, when William Bennett's horse threw him and killed him in Green Lanes, there was a woman passing, a man working in the fields and two other men hedging to be called on for help.

Commons and Eventual Enclosure

In 1528 over half of the 20 square miles of Sutton Coldfield was common or waste land. This land did not belong to any individual, but people living in Sutton had rights relating to it. The charter of 1528 specified some of these rights and gave the corporation powers to regulate the commons. Previously the commons had been administered as part of Sutton Chase, but Bishop Vesey was able to dissolve or 'disforest' the chase, making it more freely available for the grazing of sheep and other animals. The charter gave the inhabitants the right of free warren, and the right to collect firing and underwood

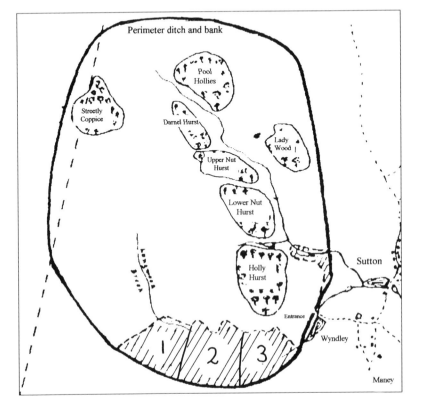

Plan showing the 60-acre farms taken out of the park, based on the late Norman Evans's plan of Sutton Park at the time of Bishop Vesey. The corporation had sold land on the southern edge of the park by 1550. (1) is Old Park Farm; (2) is Booth's Farm and (3) is Stonehouse Farm.

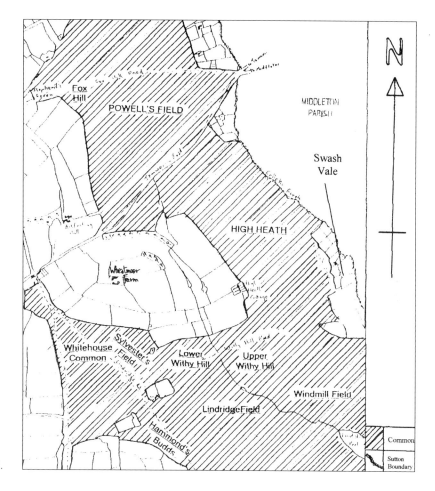

The eastern commons of Sutton Coldfield. The map shows clusters of small fields near the parish boundary and some small 'islands' of cultivated land surrounded by common. Wheatmoor Farm may be an example of a 60-acre estate taken in under the clause in the charter. The base map is the Corn Rent map of 1824.

subject to approval from the warden and society. The series of court rolls which survive from Tudor times, and later ones from the eighteenth century, record the measures taken to regulate the commons. There were orders preventing strangers from bringing their animals on to the commons, banning ploughing and controlling hunting, and fines for removing too much wood; the numbers of sheep were rationed to prevent overgrazing, and orders given for maintaining the boundary hedges.

There was more than enough common land (including the park) to meet the needs of the small population in 1528. The charter contained a clause designed to make better use of the commons and to attract enterprising newcomers to help the town to flourish: 'As often as any . . . person . . . intending there to inhabit, shall build . . . a new house . . . in the waste land of the said lordship, that they may freely and

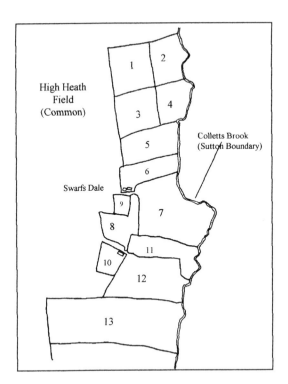

Plan of Swash Vale, redrawn from the Corporation Survey of 1811. The group of small fields and cottages on the far side of the commons probably originated as squatters' holdings. William Taylor lived at one of the 'Swarfs Dale' cottages and had fields numbered 1–4, all about three-quarters of an acre in size. George Oreton had the meadows numbered 5–7, totalling 3 acres, while 8 was his garden. He had the right-hand cottage at Swarfs Dale, described as a 'house and weaving shop', showing that he (or a predecessor) had adapted the premises for a cottage industry. Each of the other numbered holdings was tenanted by a different person.

lawfully do so . . . and enclose with ditches, hedges or pales sixty acres of the waste or less . . . to have and hold to them and their heirs for ever', paying an annual rent to the corporation of 2d per acre. Most of the yeomen and husbandmen in Sutton had farms of well below 60 acres in extent, so this represented a great opportunity for anyone with some capital and initiative. At least one new farm is recorded as being established under this clause, at Stonehouse Farm on the south side of Sutton Park, and a number of others can be inferred. The new farms tended to be set up on the best and most accessible common land, to the alarm of the existing townsmen, and in 1580 the clause was rescinded by a commissioner who ordered that only those established in the bishop's lifetime should remain, and no further ones should be made.

The commons also attracted settlers of another kind: vagrants who exercised squatter's rights here, building a rudimentary shelter to gain a foothold and consolidating if they could make a living. By the seventeenth century there were over a hundred cottages in Sutton, with concentrations in the area between Mill Street and Trinity Hill (which may once have been Great Sutton's village green), at Reddicap Heath, at Hill Hook and at the parish boundaries near Watford Gap, Slade Lane

Longmoor Mill.

and Swash Vale. Almost all the cottages paid a rent to the corporation, indicating that the land they were built on had originally been public or common land. Many of them had perhaps been there since medieval times, but the Hearth Tax return for 1670, with its entry 'Howses upon the Common that receive Collection 30', seems to identify at least thirty relatively new settlers (that is, since 1528). The warden and society periodically took measures to limit the numbers of cottages, and even to evict tenants and demolish their hovels, but in spite of this new squatters occasionally gained a foothold, often by moving into an extension of an existing cottage. Many of the cottages were occupied by widows and elderly people no longer able to work. They were often helped by the corporation, which had a considerable income from its property.

The corporation's income was increased every time any part of the commons or park was transferred to private owners or tenants, as rent then became due. Sometimes large areas of common were lost to private owners; for example, the Pudseys and Jessons of Langley were allowed to make Langley Mill Pool (1602) and Lindridge Pool (1698) to improve the water supply to Langley Mill. In the eighteenth century the new mills established in Sutton Park each had a few acres of land to farm as well as the several acres occupied by the new pools. New fields could occasionally be established on the commons, especially next to existing farmland, subject to local agreement. The most frequent way of losing parts of the common was by encroachment, where someone with property next to the common would take in a few square yards to add to their garden or to use as a saw-pit or to carry out some other process needing open space. In addition to this gradual depletion of the commons, at least 300 acres was always required for the lot acres.

The origin of the lot acres is obscure, but the practice seems to have been in force by 1600. The warden and society would designate parts of the common for cultivation by the inhabitants of the various quarters, and set out markers to divide the ground into numbered areas of an acre. Each householder would then draw a lottery ticket to find out which was his acre, the poorest person having exactly the same entitlement as the wealthiest. This acre could then be cultivated for five years, after which it reverted to common, and the warden and society would designate different parts of the commons for lot acres for the next five years. By 1800 the number of households had more than doubled, and 700 acres needed to be allotted to meet their entitlement. In the sixteenth century there were still some coppice woodlands on the commons, bounded by hedges and banks to keep the grazing animals out, where local people could harvest small timber and underwood under licence from the warden and society, but these had mostly reverted to common by the middle of the seventeenth century, leaving the extensive woods in Sutton Park to satisfy local needs.

The warden and society secured a ruling from the Lord Chancellor in 1682 forbidding any further destruction of the commons. However, this injunction also forbade any cultivation of the commons, and in 1683 a petition to the Lord Chancellor, asking for the injunction to be modified so that the system of lot acres could continue, was drawn up and signed by 145 of the 'most substantial freeholders and inhabitants'. The petition notes that 'all tillage upon the said commons and waste ground hath been forborne ever since the said injunction was granted to the great loss and prejudice of all the inhabitants in general and almost to the utter ruin and undoing of the poorer sort of people for want of corn'. This vivid illustration of the value of the lot acres is supported by evidence from the probate records. For example, in 1690 Thomas Patterton of Walmley, yeoman, had a lot acre, newly ploughed and manured, valued at 10s, the rest of his arable produce altogether being worth only £2.

Throughout the eighteenth century the warden and society continued to regulate the use of the commons and the park, which came under more pressure as the population increased. By 1800 over 700 acres had to be set out as lot acres to satisfy the increased number of households. The value of the commons was a topic of national debate, particularly as the general adoption of convertible husbandry (alternating between arable and pasture) showed that productivity could be increased if the commons were converted to farmland. In many places the conversion of the old open fields into a patchwork of square fields with hedges (a process known as enclosure) was achieved by act of Parliament, and in the eighteenth century local acts of Parliament for the enclosure of commons began to be passed. Enclosure of the commons involved allocating areas of common to private individuals according to their assessed entitlement, which then became their property to exploit as they chose. All the rights of common formerly enjoyed by the local people were extinguished, but the more productive farming of the new land increased the wealth of the community as a whole, made farmers more prosperous and gave more employment opportunities to those without any land of their own. The process was controversial, however, and a proposal for the enclosure of Sutton Coldfield commons put forward in 1778 caused an uproar, as no one wanted to lose their rights of common and lot acres, or to see the park converted to farmland.

In 1791 a paper was published showing the advantages of enclosure in Sutton Coldfield: 'Instead of the half-starved race of sheep, cattle and horses with which these commons are at present stored [they] will abound with superior numbers of a more profitable race of each of these species of animals, besides a produce of bread and beer for multitudes of human creatures.' The commons (including the park) were described as 'covered with ling, furze or herbage, for the most part very indifferent', and it would require a considerable outlay, perhaps £11 per acre, to make the land productive. The rector, John Riland, opposed enclosure of the commons, partly on the grounds that it would be unfair to the poor, but one of the most drastic effects of enclosure does not appear to have been articulated at the time. The poor cottager enjoyed rights on the commons shared with all his neighbours, rich and poor, and he had the option, if no satisfactory work was available, of scavenging on the common for fuel, tending his sheep or tilling his lot acre. After the commons were enclosed, he had no option but to work for a wage, on the land or in a factory. From being a free man, he had become a wage slave.

By 1824 all the neighbouring parishes had enclosed, the corporation was no longer under the eye of the Court of Chancery and the new rector favoured enclosure. The growth of population locally and nationally was putting a strain on the limited amount of commons, which were always difficult to police, and so the majority of the freeholders of Sutton were now in favour of enclosing the commons. Accordingly, an act of Parliament was obtained for the enclosure of the commons and those parts

The Tithe Barn in High Street, supposed to have been built by Bishop Vesey using some of the decorative stones from the old manor house. This photograph was taken in 1855 by William Grundy, a pioneer photographer who lived in the Georgian house to the right of the picture, now the Royal Hotel. (*Norman Evans Collection*)

of the open fields in Wigginshill which were still unenclosed, and a commissioner was appointed to undertake the task. The act provided for the tithes, which were payable in kind, to be converted to monetary payments. The tithes were payable to the rector, who had a tithe barn in High Street where he could store one-tenth of every crop grown in Sutton, which was his due. He was also entitled to a proportion of all livestock born in the parish. The commissioner's first task was to identify the owners of all the property in Sutton Coldfield, and establish the extent of their holdings. He found that there were 255 owners of land and property, who owned between them 7,081 acres; there were only 32 owners of over 50 acres, but 124 with less than 5 acres.

SEVEN
The Commons Enclosed

By 1824 there had been over a thousand Parliamentary acts for the enclosure of commons in England. The procedure was well established, and the work began immediately. The enclosure commissioner's first task had been to establish for the Corn Rent (the conversion of tithes to a money rent) exactly who the owners were and precise the extent of their property. By doing this, he determined the amount of land in private ownership, and could assume that the remainder (excluding the park) was common land, available to be enclosed and allotted. However, the commons so defined were not of a uniform nature as regards their history, potential value, fertility, convenience of location and need for capital investment. Nor were they evenly distributed across Sutton, including as they did the vast open expanses that comprised most of the acreage; local patches of land of the village green type; wide road-side verges and a few special cases.

The process of enclosure has been studied at Four Oaks. In 1824 this hamlet consisted of eighteen dwellings clustered along a village green at the junction of Four Oaks Road and Belwell Lane. Sutton Park was to the west, cultivated land to the south and east, and to the north was Four Oaks Common. The inhabitants of Four Oaks enjoyed their common rights over Four Oaks Common, a stretch of about 180 acres lying between Streetly Lane and Blackberry Lane. The first act of the enclosure commissioner was to set out the roads across the trackless waste, drawn on the plan with a ruler and pencil. These were Walsall Road (30 feet wide), Streetly Lane (40 feet wide) and Crown Lane (30 feet wide). Blackberry Lane and Edge Hill Road were set out, originally as private roads. Belwell Lane and Four Oaks Road were also set out where they had previously been widened to form the village green. The commissioner was concerned with

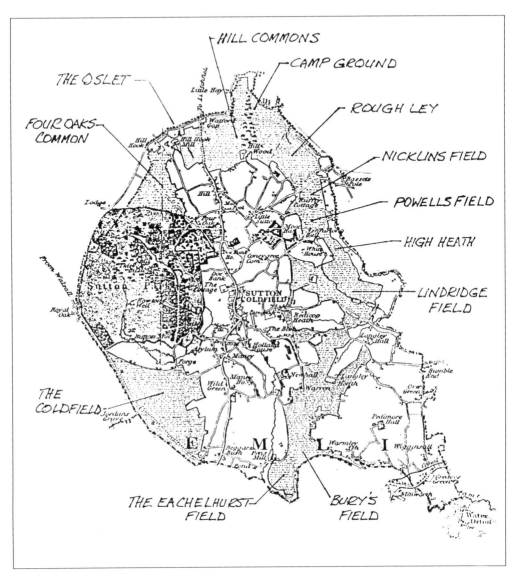

Sutton Coldfield commons as they were in 1822. The names of smaller 'fields' cannot be shown at this scale. The park with wastes and commons is represented by the shaded areas. (map by A.F. Fentiman).

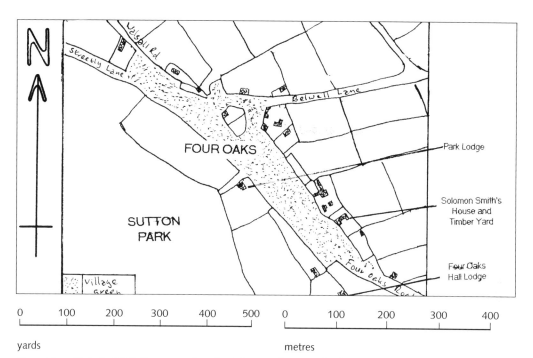

Plan of Four Oaks in 1824. Base map: Corn Rent Survey of 1824–5 for the Enclosure Commission.

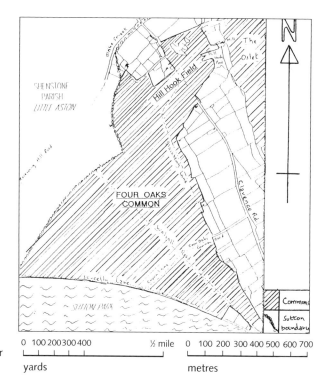

Map of Four Oaks Common.
Base map: Corn Rent Survey of 1824–5 for
the Enclosure Commission.

all the commons in Sutton, but naturally chose to allocate parts of Four Oaks Common to the local proprietors, who included the owners of Four Oaks Hall, Four Oaks Farm and a few houses between Four Oaks Farm and Four Oaks Common Road, in addition to the houses in the hamlet itself.

Solomon Smith's house, 'The Larches', in Four Oaks Road.

A total of 160 acres of Four Oaks Common went to just four owners. None of them was an inhabitant of Four Oaks. The Enclosure Act specified that the commissioner's expenses should be met by the sale of plots of the commons to be enclosed, and of the total area of 3,330 acres of commons in Sutton over 900 were sold to defray his expenses. At Four Oaks 90 acres were sale plots, most of them north of Four Oaks Common Road; these were purchased by Thomas Edge, who built himself a big house at Edge Hill and set up as a gentleman farmer. The rector received 42 acres in lieu of tithes, and Sir E.C. Hartopp of Four Oaks Hall also received 42 acres (31 of them by purchase). Most of this land was used to form a new farm of 68 acres with its farmhouse on Streetly Lane. Thomas Rochford, the owner of Four Oaks Farm, received 18 acres to add to his farm, lying between his farmland and Streetly Lane.

The proprietors at the hamlet of Four Oaks received parts of the former village green in fourteen different lots, mostly in front of their existing property, totalling nearly 3 acres. Those who were entitled to additional land were allotted small plots near Four Oaks Common Road. Only one of the Four Oaks owners, Solomon Smith, took advantage of the process to improve his holding. He bought the entitlements of four of his neighbours and a small sale plot and obtained a block of 9 acres south of

Crown Lane. Those who lived in Four Oaks but did not own property received nothing to compensate them for their loss of privileges on the common, although they still enjoyed rights in Sutton Park. Thus the inhabitants of Four Oaks, who had previously enjoyed rights of common over 180 acres of land, were between them only entitled to allotments of less than 10 acres in total.

Many of those who received allotments of less than an acre in a part of the common a long way from their existing property could make little use of them. The cost of fencing alone would be hard to recover, and so many people sold their entitlement. More substantial owners also received allotments that were awkwardly placed, but for them the Enclosure Act offered a unique opportunity. If they could reach an agreement with another owner, they could propose an exchange of lands to the commissioner; if he agreed and included it in his eventual award, this would give both parties absolute title to their exchanged lands without the inconvenience of a formal conveyance. At Four Oaks Bishop Vesey's Grammar School owned a small field and received a small allotment; the governors agreed with the rector to exchange this and some other land in return for 11 acres of the rector's land next to the main body of the school property south of Tamworth Road. Other substantial owners who took advantage of this clause to build up their estates were Sir Francis Lawley of Canwell, Andrew Hackett of Moxhall, the Websters of Penns and Bagot of Pype Hayes.

The various parts of the commons were named. The common north-east of Four Oaks Common was Hill Hook Field, and to the east of that lay The Oslet. The commons continued in an unbroken swathe round north-east Sutton to Lindridge Field in the east. To the south of this the commons were still continuous, but they had been subject to more settlement and encroachment, giving the impression of open space between farmland rather than the great expanses of the northern commons. Reddicap Heath and Bull's Field both had more the appearance of large greens than open common. This great arc of commons ended with Echelhurst Field south of Walmley, where the E brook formed the boundary with Erdington. To the south of Sutton Park was another very extensive tract of common, where Boldmere is now, which was then known simply as The Coldfield. This name originally applied to the extensive heathland which once extended through Kingstanding to Barr Beacon, nearly to Aldridge, and included Streetly and Four Oaks Common (see pages 90 and 100–3).

It was on these large areas of common that new estates could be established, for example at Fox Hill and Falcon Lodge, and new farms could be laid out as

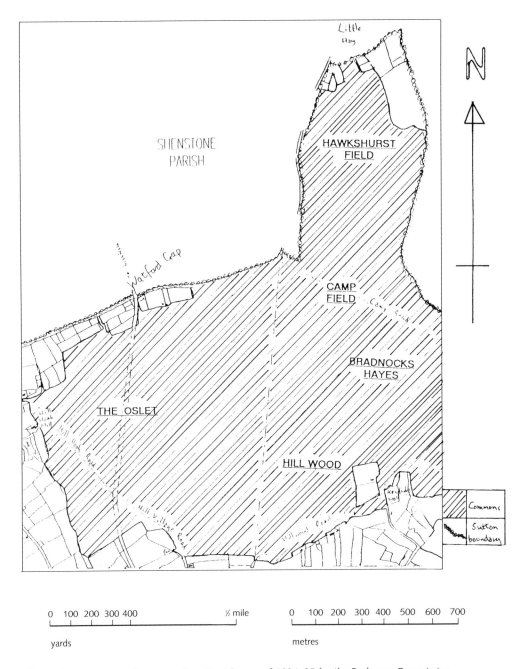

The northern commons. Base map: Corn Rent Survey of 1824–25 for the Enclosure Commission.

The north-eastern commons. Base map: Corn Rent Survey of 1824–5 for the Enclosure Commission.

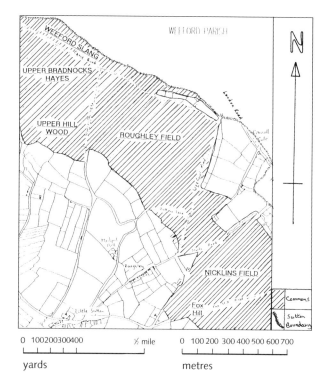

The eastern commons. Base map: Corn Rent Survey of 1824–5 for the Enclosure Commission.

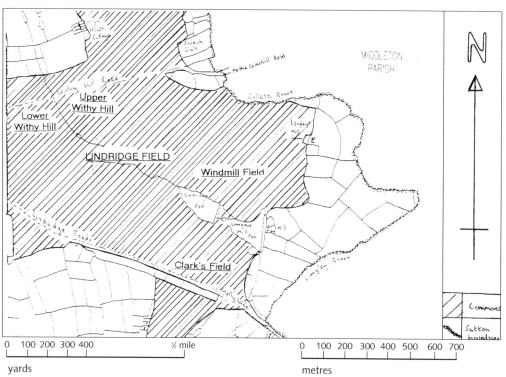

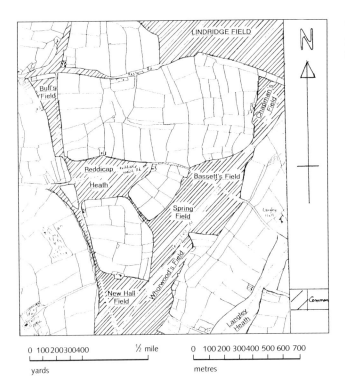

The south-eastern commons. Base map: Corn Rent Survey of 1824–5 for the Enclosure Commission.

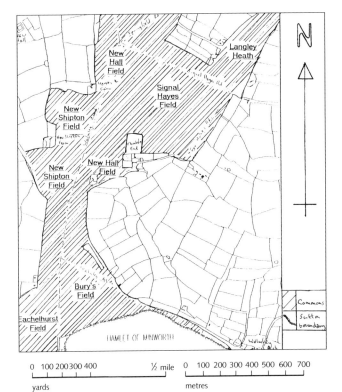

The commons at Walmley. Base map: Corn Rent Survey of 1824–5 for the Enclosure Commission.

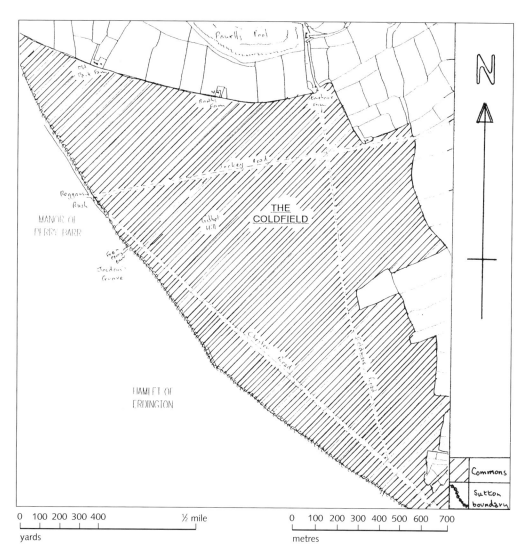

The Coldfield Common (Boldmere). Base map: Corn Rent Survey of 1824–25 for the Enclosure Commission.

at Streetly Lane and Manorial Farm. The latter, in Hillwood Road, belonged to the corporation, which had received over 100 acres of allotments in return for surrendering income previously received as lords of the manor. This allotment was therefore known as the manorial allotment. Having laid out the farm, they advertised for a tenant in the *Midland Counties Herald* in 1832. Such new farms needed

Manorial Farm.

considerable investment (estimated at £11 per acre), both to bring the land into good heart and for the farm buildings and equipment. In some cases they proved not to be viable, either through lack of investment or because of insufficient land. The ruins of the original Withy Hill Farm, now re-established on another site and farming more land, could be seen until recently, and showed that the buildings were of poor quality.

Withy Hill Farm. (*Janet Lillywhite*)

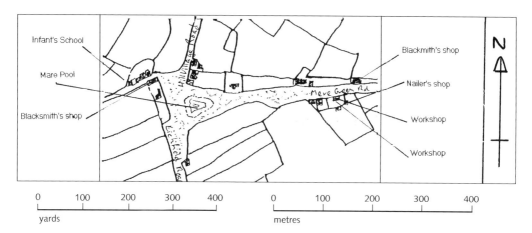

Mere Green in 1824.

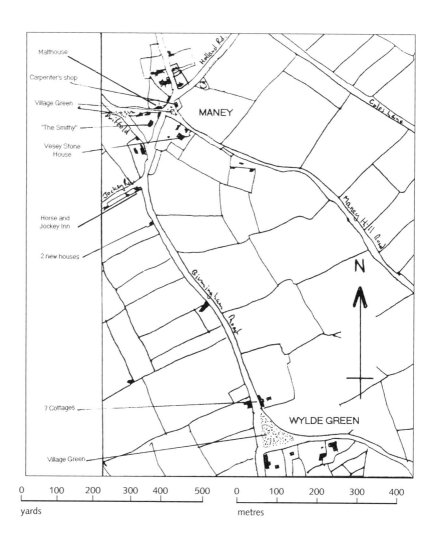

Maney and
Wylde Green in
1824.
Base map: Corn
Rent Survey
of 1824–5 for
the Enclosure
Commission.

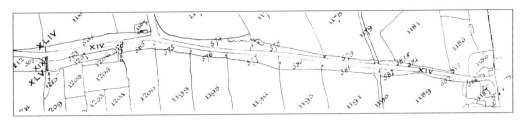

Ox Leys Road. The new enclosure road (XIV) with its hedges 30-feet apart replaced the old wide road. Most of the old hedgebanks have been ploughed out, but some survive.

The enclosure saw the end of eleven village greens in Sutton, ranging from the small greens at Hill and Maney to the more extensive ones at Four Oaks, Mere Green, Over Wishaw Green and Minworth Greaves. Usually small pieces of former green were added to the gardens or fields of neighbouring properties. At Four Oaks new houses were built in front of the old building line at the edge of the green, but at Little Sutton the present building line preserves the shape of the old village green, though no old houses survive. Mere Green gradually supplanted Hill and Little Sutton as the focus for the north of Sutton, while the former green at Wylde Green hardly developed at all. In the south the new centres at Boldmere and Walmley were both new sites, established alongside the roads laid out across the former commons by the enclosure commissioner. The old roads to Langley, Bulls Lane and Ox Leys Road did not escape; new roads 30 feet wide were set out, and the verges to either side were added to the adjacent fields.

Ox Leys Road. This is the field marked 574 on the map above, which was a marlpit within the width of the old road before enclosure. The overgrown pre-enclosure hedge is on the left, the newer (1825) hedge is on the right.

Size of Allotment	No. of allottees
Under 1 acre	78
1 - 4 acres	88
5 - 9 acres	19
10 - 19 acres	16
20 - 39 acres	9
40 - 99 acres	10
Over 100 acres	1

Table of allotments showing that most proprietors received very small allotments of common.

Enclosure award title page.

Aerial view at Hillwood Common Road, showing the rectangular enclosure fields.

Four Oaks Road, laid out at enclosure with a width of 30 feet, is now too narrow to allow a pavement on each side.

The enclosure of the commons was almost complete by 1830, and most of the new owners were developing their new land before then. The complexities of accommodating some of the 255 different owners, some of whom were hard to trace, and satisfying the various appeals and queries which arose, took much longer, and the final award did not appear until 1851. This document (see page 107), with the Corn Rent schedule, is very informative. The corn rent map is a large-scale plan of Sutton made in 1824–5 showing every field and house, all numbered so that a description can be found in the accompanying schedule. The blank spaces on this map, representing areas not in private ownership, were portioned off by the commissioner to show the various allotments, also numbered and identified in a schedule in the award of 1851. For the first time we have an accurate description of every square yard of Sutton Coldfield.

The face of Sutton was changed by enclosure. The commissioner's division of the commons into allotment fields was done very precisely, and the geometric pattern this imposed on the landscape can still be seen. This patchwork of rectangular fields was very marked in some areas, especially where a large number of small holdings were concentrated, since many of the new fields were very small; over 150 were under 5 acres. Even in areas which are now built-up the work of the enclosure commissioner lives on in the straight roads which he laid out; many of them are still confined to the 30-foot width specified in the award – an ample width at the time, but far too narrow now.

EIGHT
New Challenges for Local Government

In the same year as the Enclosure Act of 1824, the Court of Chancery approved a scheme which ensured that the corporation's income was used for the public good. The scheme was put into practice by the warden and society without delay, and new life and vigour seem to have come into their proceedings. The warden and society appointed committees to deal with the issues arising from the enclosure, to establish new schools and to consider the management of the cottages (after enclosure of the commons, the corporation had taken over full ownership and responsibility for the cottages). Other committees were set up as needed. This was a more business-like body than the one which had spent long hours in the 1780s arguing over the granting of hunting rights in Sutton Park. The resolution of the Chancery case appeared to have given the charter a new stamp of approval, and the old corporation a new lease of life. However, there were other forces at work which gradually undermined the warden and society over the next sixty years.

The Great Reform Act of 1832, which made parliamentary constituencies more representative of the population and widened the franchise, was passed after widespread campaigning throughout the country. Annual rallies had been held in Birmingham, the one in 1832 being attended by an estimated 200,000 people. The Great Reform Act was followed by a movement for municipal reform. In 1835 the constitution of ancient boroughs was reviewed, and Sutton Coldfield was one of the boroughs called to account before a commission. The deputy steward (equivalent to a town clerk), Thomas Holbeche, gave evidence to the effect that the town was well governed, that it had recently been vetted by the Court of Chancery and that the inhabitants were content with their corporation and the way it was constituted. The rector also appeared before the commission. He painted a slightly less rosy picture of the general attitude to the self-elected warden and society, but agreed that it was functioning satisfactorily. Sutton Coldfield was one of just 7 places (out of 246 reviewed) not included in the subsequent Municipal Corporations Act.

Although there were no local government elections in Sutton, there was an opportunity to vote at the general elections, when the two members of Parliament for North Warwickshire were to be elected. In the 1830s Sutton voted strongly in favour of the conservatives, Dugdale and Wilmot; in 1835 the radical Gregory received 40 votes in Sutton compared with 157 and 128 for Dugdale and Wilmot. These votes were cast at Coleshill, but Sutton became a polling place in 1837, as Helen Holbeche (who lived at the Old Rectory) recalled:

> At the elections the polling booths were opposite our house, by the old Town Hall, the Conservative colours were orange and green (Wilmott and Dugdale), and dishes of fruit were sent over to the clerks, decorated with marigolds and green leaves. Our two eldest sisters receiving silk handkerchiefs of these colours from the successful candidate Sir E. Wilmott. His son sleeping at our house, we got our windows broken in consequence. Next house to us lived a hot radical doctor, who hung out a blue flag.

The old workhouse in Mill Street.

Relief of the poor in the eighteenth century was administered by the churchwardens, but the corporation was ultimately responsible for it under the 1601 Poor Law Act. Under the Workhouse Test Act of 1722 the parish was empowered to build a workhouse to accommodate the able-bodied poor. The workhouse in Mill Street was built in 1737, on the site of the original Bishop Vesey Grammar School, with an endowment of land at Riland Road called The Blabbs, but afterwards known as Workhouse Meadow. The 1824 scheme included the provision of almshouses for the poor, but did not alter the management of the workhouse, which was now controlled by a body known as the Select Vestry. A new act of Parliament in 1834 established a new system for the administration of the poor law which grouped parishes together into Poor Law Unions, and the Sutton poor with their workhouse were administered by the Aston Board of Guardians from 1836. The workhouse at Sutton closed in 1837 and its inmates transferred to the Union workhouse in Erdington.

The role of local government in the new industrial age was emphasised locally by the granting of a borough charter to Birmingham in 1839. Previously governed by a ramshackle arrangement of street commissioners, lords of the manor and parish officials, it now had an elected mayor and corporation. Sutton had seemed well governed by comparison, but now it was the warden and society that began to be seen as an anachronism. Although still a predominantly agricultural market town, Sutton had a growing population, and a proportion of this increase was made up of manufacturers and businessmen from the neighbouring industrial towns who came to live in Sutton. The newcomers felt entitled to be treated as equals, but they found a closed corporation to which they had no access. They also found that the corporation, struggling to come to terms with the growth in population, was restricting access to some of the attractions of Sutton that the newcomers had come to enjoy, especially the pursuit of game in Sutton Park. Over-exploitation had already destroyed most of the game, but fury at being turned out of the park was the catalyst for a new attack on the corporation. In 1854 there was a rally of over 2,000 people disgruntled with the warden and society, and at the mass meeting it was resolved to petition the government for a new, democratic, charter.

A public enquiry was held at Sutton in the summer of 1855 to look into the case made by the petitioners for a new corporation. The zeal of the reformers had cooled in the meantime, while the warden and society had taken measures to counter the arguments and complaints raised in the petition. Their case was ably presented. None of the accusations of corrupt or improper practice could be sustained, and

The Parade and Mill Street, *c.* 1870, showing the town hall with its clock tower. In front of the town hall are some almshouses and to the right of them, behind the brand new gas lamp, is the Town School. (*Norman Evans Collection*)

their solicitor successfully challenged many of the signatures on the petition. The commissioner, Major Warburton, reported that the warden and society were not in need of reform. This conclusion was reached partly thanks to some particularly able and energetic members of the corporation at this time, such as B.D. Webster, who was warden five times. He oversaw the building of a new Town Hall on Mill Street (opened in 1859), and was a prime mover in bringing the railway to Sutton.

In 1859 the warden and society disagreed on the question of which railway line to support. The line Webster favoured, to the east of Birmingham Road, had been put forward as a result of Webster's discussions with his fellow guardians at the Aston Union, his fellow trustees on various Turnpike Trusts, his fellow freemasons, his fellow huntsmen and his business acquaintances. Such informal networks were at least as influential as the formal machinery of local government in framing policy and reaching decisions in an age before party politics came to predominate. The warden and society took a vote on the railway issue. Webster declared his interest and abstained; although almost all the others stood to make personal gains depending on which line was built, they voted anyway. Their decision to support the Western line made little difference to the eventual result. The fact that some of them made a fortune when the line was built reinforced the suspicions of those who felt that the closed corporation was working for the interests of its own members rather than for the town it governed.

In 1853 Sutton received a request from the mayor of Birmingham to grant part of the park so that a pleasure resort for the general public could be built there. This was to be especially for the working classes of Birmingham who rarely saw a tree or drew a breath of clear air. The request was declined, on the grounds that the warden and society were custodians of the park as a public open space, and therefore could not agree to lease any part of it to any other body. This high-minded stance was recalled by local people when a proposal for a railway through the park was put forward. A petition signed by 194 inhabitants urged the corporation to oppose the plan. The warden and society met on 17 February 1872 and duly resolved to oppose the railway through the park, appointing an executive committee to carry out this resolution. However, the committee failed to oppose the bill in Parliament, and the corporation left subsequent opposition to others. It gradually became clear that the majority of its members were shareholders of the new railway or stood to gain financially if it was built, and from this time dissatisfaction with the warden and society became widespread and bitter.

Unreformed municipal corporations were the subject of a national enquiry in 1876. The increased population of Sutton caused new and contentious problems. New laws giving local authorities responsibility for drainage, town planning and refuse collection had been enacted, but the warden and society were unable to implement them as the Aston Union was considered to be the relevant authority. There was even a proposal for the Union to appoint a Sutton Coldfield sub-committee. The warden and society now supported their own dissolution and replacement by a modern authority. A new charter came into force in 1886 bringing to an end the 357 years of their existence. In spite of all the complaints, the warden and society had introduced free education for all as early as 1825, had used their considerable income to alleviate the hardships of the poor, and appointed a parish surgeon as early as 1834 to attend the 'in and out' poor. It was only when the increased population and prosperity of the 1870s brought social and economic stress that the old corporation with its limited powers proved unable to cope.

The new Municipal Charter for Sutton Coldfield provided for a democratically elected corporation, with six wards each electing three councillors and an alderman. The resulting corporation of twenty-four men elected a mayor from among themselves. The new authority took on all the powers and duties set out in the Municipal Corporations Act of 1882, and in particular the responsibility for public health and planning, both previously undertaken by the Aston Union. Committees were established to report on various aspects of the corporation's work, including

Health and Highways; Park, Estates and Buildings; Finance; and General Purposes; in 1888 the new Fire Brigade and Hackney Carriages Committee was introduced.

The old corporation had owned a large amount of property, the proceeds of which had to be devoted to charitable works. This charity property was excluded from the powers of the new corporation, and put instead into the hands of the trustees of the Sutton Coldfield Municipal Charities. A large proportion of the property was educational, including all the school buildings as well as the endowed property earmarked for educational purposes. The schools were administered by a School Board, on which the corporation was strongly represented, but other bodies also served on the board, which was answerable to the Government Department of Education. The old corporation had had its own education committee as well as looking after the charitable works – almshouses, poor maidens' portions, lying-in charities, widows' payments, and so on – and was advised by a Ladies' Committee. This committee left no records, but the warden and society minutes sometimes refer to its recommendations. The Ladies' Committee was made up of educated gentlewomen, spinsters such as the five Misses Holbeche, the three Misses Bracken, the two Misses Cull, the two Misses Webb and Miss Grundy, as well as the wives and daughters of the leading men of the town. It may have been a considerable power behind the scenes, for its members certainly undertook charitable work such as visiting the sick and assisting in schools.

The charitable work of the corporation was described at the 1855 enquiry by the deputy steward, Mr Holbeche:

Almshouses at Walmley.

I think I may mention that from childhood to old age, during the whole of a man's life, he receives benefit from the funds of the warden and society. For instance, as you are aware, childbed linen is provided for the use of the poor married women, and a surgeon to attend them in childbed; the children are vaccinated; they are sent to the schools; they are clothed; they are put out to apprentices, or the girls to service, with new clothes; and girls, you have been told, if good characters, receive marriage portions of £24 each. There are about 100 cottages in the parish, some without land attached, some with a garden, and some with three or four acres of land; the most meritorious poor inhabitants are usually elected tenants of these places. Blankets are annually distributed to the poor. During manhood they have the pasturage, fern, gorse, ling, broken branches of timber and fuel for their fires. The poor, in old age, are placed in alms houses, with an allowance of 15s a month for a single man or woman, and 25s for a married man and his wife, and 30 cwt. of coal a year.

Only four members of the old corporation were elected to the new one, giving the new corporation the added vigour brought by new men. By 1903 the new corporation had gained more control over education, and also had committees for electric lighting, school attendance, technical education and cemeteries, as well as having successfully lobbied for a Crown Court. Although the corporation took pride in its services such as schools, electricity and highways, it was in some degree paternalistic. The population in 1885 was estimated as 8,000, but that figure had more than quadrupled to 33,000 by 1935. The growing population included a considerable working-class component. When the working men's club inquired in 1908 as to what progress the corporation had made in securing a tramway for Sutton, the reply came that the time was not yet ripe. Indoor public baths were not considered necessary until 1970, and Sutton did not adopt the Public Libraries Act until 1938, one of the last authorities in the country to do so. The population of Sutton continued to grow in the second half of the twentieth century, and the corporation continued to provide appropriate services, but without attracting modern development and dynamism to the town centre. Despite the extensive re-development which was under way by 1972, and a vigorous campaign to retain its independence, Sutton Coldfield was not granted metropolitan borough status in the Local Government Act of 1974. Sutton became part of the new Birmingham authority, and the town's four and a half centuries of independence came to an end.

NINE

Transport

In the eighteenth century anyone travelling to London by coach from Sutton would need to allow at least three days for the journey. Local journeys would be quickest on horseback, but most people travelled on foot. In the sixteenth century a poor man set off from Sutton Coldfield, arriving at Bridgnorth with the help of a ride in a farmer's cart; the next day he walked to Cressage and the next day to Shrewsbury. In Shrewsbury he was tried as a vagrant, found guilty and hanged, so poor travellers were in peril from the law as well as the hardships of the open road. As a young man in 1728 Dr Johnson often walked from Lichfield to Birmingham in the morning, returning on foot at night, perhaps calling on his uncle Nicholas Ford in Sutton Coldfield on the way. Later in the century Dr Alcock would travel from Lichfield to Sutton on horseback every Sunday to play the organ at the parish church. The cost of hiring a horse in 1784 was 2s.

One reason for the lack of a more efficient way of travelling was the poor state of the roads, which were often almost impassable in bad weather. It was the responsibility of the parish to maintain roads, but there was no obligation or incentive to make improvements. However, in 1792 the roads in Sutton Coldfield must have been in particularly bad condition, as the warden and society spent £350 improving the streets of the town by paving them with cobblestones, and 'the high roads from Watford Gap to Chester Road and from Canwell to Sutton were placed under trustees, and toll gates erected at the north end of Sutton, at Ashfurlong, and at Collet's Brook'. If this trust was indeed set up in 1792 (it has left no records), and was empowered to manage the roads and charge tolls, it would have ensured that the roads were brought up to a better standard because the necessary capital works could then have been undertaken.

The old tollhouse at Collet's Brook, Tamworth Road.

Indifputable REASONS

AGAINST THE

Propofed Scheme for a TURNPIKE ROAD,

Between SUTTON and BIRMINGHAM.

TURNPIKE Acts are always undefirable, except where Neceffity compels their Eftablifhment. A large Proportion of the Tolls is ever funk upon what does not a whit Benefit the Travellers. Gates, Houfes, Sa-laries for Keepers, Clerks, endlefs Advertifements, and the enormous Exactions attend-ing the procuring the Act.----Befides an opening is continually afforded for clandef-tine Jobs, which the vulgar Phrafe of " You fcratch me, and I'll fcratch you," will, in a fhorter Manner, at leaft, explain, than the Recital of Particulars.

But—peculiar local Objections offer themfelves againft the Plan now on Foot : ---- The whole Road which can be called foundrous or dangerous is not four Miles ; and it is believed no Inftance can be given where the Legiflature hath interfered for fo fmall an Object. Thefe four Miles moreover are encompaffed with Inclofures whofe Value, upon an Average, is encreafed from One Pound to Two per Acre, merely up-on Account of their Vicinity to the Highway in Queftion, it being an Avenue to the Town of Birmingham.----That thefe Land-Owners then fhould tacitly enjoy the Afflu-ence which that Vicinage gives them, and yet be permitted to fhift off the local In-convenience of extraordinary road-mending from their own fat Shoulders to the Back of the Farmer, the Scotch or Irifh Traveller, whom Birmingham never profited a Brafs Farthing ; is a Manœuvre which may be very pleafant in the Contrivance, and clever in the Execution, but what no Reprefentatives of the Nation will, furely allow.

Part of a broadside (a single-sheet political leaflet).

The establishment of the local trust in 1792 had been opposed in a printed broadside issued by some Sutton farmers 'from the plough tail', on the grounds that the existing roads were good enough for their purposes, and the imposition of tolls on the passage of farm animals would be ruinous to the poorer farmers. Vehicles using turnpike roads were required by law to comply with certain standards, which the poor farmers of Sutton could not afford to meet. This made it difficult for them to cart muck from Birmingham, to the great loss of fertility of their land, and they feared that the wealthier farmers with their 'Parliament wheels' would 'engross all the muck'.

For a trust to function properly, it needed to be established as a Turnpike Trust by act of Parliament. The first Turnpike Act for the Sutton roads was passed in 1807, covering the present A5127 from Chester Road to Watford Gap and the A453 Tamworth Road. The preamble to this act, which explains why it is necessary, mentions that the existing trustees had insufficient powers to improve the condition

Certain Lands and Buildings to be taken for the Purposes of the Act.

XXXII. And be it further enacted, That it shall be lawful for the said Trustees, or any Five or more of them, to take so much of a Piece or Parcel of Land now used as a Garden, situate on the Western Side of the said Road leading from *Birmingham* to *Lichfield*, belonging to the Masters, Fellows, and Scholars of *Emanuel* College, in the University of *Cambridge*, in the Occupation of *Samuel Waddam*, as will range in a strait Line from a certain Building now used as a Blacksmith's Shop, situate at or near to the Bottom of the said Town of *Sutton Colfield*, now in the Occupation of the said *Samuel Waddam* or his Undertenant, to a certain Building, now used as a stable, belonging to *Andrew Hacket* Esquire, in the Occupation of *Edward Sadler* Gentleman ; and also to take so much of the Land belonging to the said Warden and Society of the Royal Town of *Sutton Coldfield*, at or near to the Bottom of the said Town of *Sutton Coldfield*, now used as a Garden, and in the Occupation of *Joseph James*, lying on the Eastern Side of the said Road leading from *Birmingham* to *Lichfield*, as shall be necessary ; and also to take down a certain Pig Stye or Hovel belonging to the said Warden and Society, in the Occupation of *Thomas Norris*, and to take the Land on which the same is erected, and so much of the Land occupied therewith as shall be necessary ; and also to take down a certain Building occupied with and adjoining to a Messuage, Cottage, or Tenement belonging to the said Warden and Society, in the Occupation of *John Farmer*, adjoining to the said last-mentioned Land, as shall be necessary; and also take down such Part of a certain Messuage, Cottage, or Tenement, and Pig Stye, and to take the Land on which such Part of the said Buildings

Extract from the Birmingham & Watford Gap Turnpike Act of 1807.

Part of the Corn Rent map of 1824, showing the realigned Turnpike Road (now The Parade) crossing fields nos 796, 797 and 798 on an embankment to the foot of Mill Street, and continuing in a direct line up Mill Street, the buildings and gardens which obstructed the route having been cleared away. The newly laid-out Park Road is also shown, cutting across field no. 801.

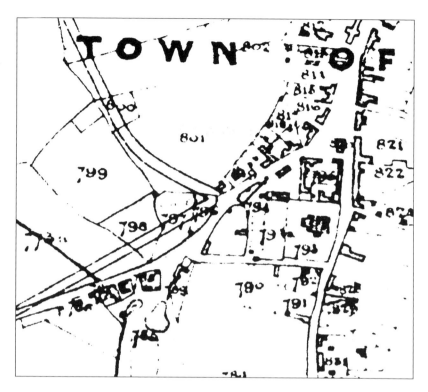

of the roads, which were in 'so ruinous a condition as to be unsafe for the passage of cattle and carriages'. By 1807 turnpike roads were well established all over England, and the mail coach from London to Birmingham made the journey in 12 hours, a great improvement over the two days taken in 1750. Accurate surveying methods had been perfected in the eighteenth century, but the technique of building roads with proper foundations and a metalled surface was poorly developed.

The Turnpike Act was renewed in 1817 and 1827, giving the trustees powers to make compulsory purchases of land required for improvements. The main works were at Mere Green, where a new road by-passing Hill Village was made through the farmland (the original route had been the twisting, narrow and steep Hill Village Road), and at Mill Street. The works at Mill Street were done because of the steepness and awkwardness of the hill. Straightening the road involved the demolition of a house, while the gradient was reduced by building a substantial embankment at the bottom (now The Parade) and making a cutting at the top. As Sarah Holbeche observed in her diary, '1824: the top of the town was carried to the bottom' (see above; the newly made road at Mill Street is shown on page 112).

Other road works carried out about this time were the construction of Park Road, the realignment of Four Oaks Road to allow for the expansion of Four Oaks Park and the re-routing of Little Sutton Lane. These improvements allowed the roads to carry the increasing traffic generated by the expansion of trade at the beginning of the industrial revolution.

The siting of the toll-gates on the roads was rationalised so that the only one in Sutton was in Lichfield Road near the present Holy Trinity Catholic church. The redundant toll-house at Collet's Brook was sold in 1831 and is still standing, the only surviving toll-house in Birmingham. The upper storey of the bay window facing the turnpike road has blocked-in recesses instead of side windows, where the toll boards would have been displayed which set out the charges: 2*s* for a six-horse carriage, 1*s* for a four-horse coach, 6*d* for a two-horse coach and 3*d* for a one-horse gig; 1*s* was charged for a large wagon, 9*d* for a medium wagon, 6*d* for a two-wheel cart with four horses, 4*d* with three horses, 3*d* with two horses, 2*d* with one horse; horses 1*d* each, cattle 10*d* a score and sheep 5*d* a score. In 1835 the income of the Birmingham & Watford Gap Turnpike Trust from tolls was £2,095 13*s* 8*d*. Directories for the middle of the nineteenth century give details of the regular services using the roads. In 1854 daily omnibuses from Lichfield and Tamworth to Birmingham called at the Three Tuns, those operated by Peedles ran to Birmingham three times a day and Sheppard's once; and there were two carriers offering a daily service to Birmingham.

The Birmingham & Fazeley Canal at Wigginshill Lane bridge. The area on the right is listed as a boatyard in 1856.

Other forms of transport were competing for traffic, however. The Birmingham & Fazeley Canal, which opened in 1789, passes through the south-eastern corner of Sutton, but was too far away from the town to have much impact on trade. The heavy goods carried by canals which were in demand in Sutton, such as building stone and tiles, were carted from the wharves at Aston, while coal was brought by cart from the pitheads at Brownhills. Far from seeking to be more closely connected to the canal network the warden and society showed their indifference. In 1793 they were approached by a canal company about a projected canal to link the Black Country to the Trent & Mersey Canal, with a possible route through Sutton. The response given (11 March 1793) was that the corporation had no objection, so long as the canal was not within half a mile of Four Oaks Hall. Sir Edmund Hartopp, the owner of the hall, had just been made a member of the society at the time.

For a time it appeared that the same negative attitude would be taken towards railways. When a railway line to Sutton was proposed in 1853, a petition against it was signed by over 400 inhabitants who did not wish Sutton to become a 'smoky and degraded suburb of Birmingham'. But the prospect of having a railway had been generally welcomed in 1845, when a company was set up to build one which would pass through the town. The surveyor for the company (the Birmingham, Lichfield & Manchester Railway Company) was John R. McLean, one of the great early railway engineers. He reported to the board in October 1845 on two possible routes between Birmingham and Lichfield. One lay through the town of Sutton itself and the other ran to the west of Sutton Park. 'I should recommend the Sutton Coldfield line if that town were a place of much importance', he reported, 'but as I understand it has little trade, and [is] principally composed of an agricultural population, to whom rail conveyance is not essential, I would advise you to adopt the line through Sutton Park.' When news of this decision reached Sutton, a town meeting was called at the Town Hall on 14 November, where the outraged townsfolk passed an indignant resolution beginning:

This meeting has heard with surprise and regret, that after all the notices which appeared relative to the Birmingham, Lichfield & Manchester Railway Company promising in distinct terms the necessary advantages to the town of Sutton Coldfield, this line is now projected to run at a distance which will entirely preclude the inhabitants from any advantages of railway communication . . .

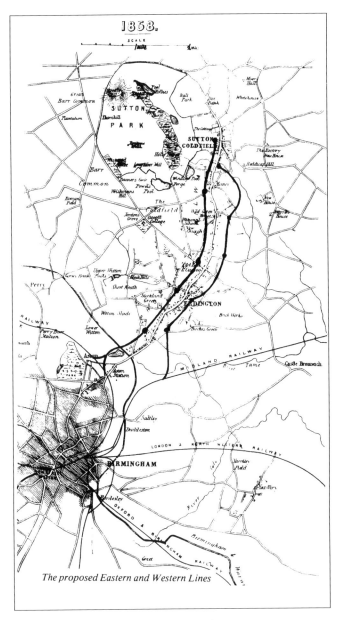

The proposed Eastern and Western Lines

The proposed railway routes to Sutton, 1858.

The strong support for a railway to Sutton now being shown led the corporation to secure a bond from the company to make a station at Sutton. This bond was renewed in 1846 when the company was taken over by the newly formed London & North Western Railway. Their famous engineer, Joseph Locke, surveyed a line through Sutton on the east side of the Turnpike Road, but then came recession and the line was never built. The penalty in the bond was invoked, and the new Town Hall on Mill Street (opened 1859) was built with the £3,000 compensation received. Other proposals were made for a line in the 1850s, but the decisive step came in 1857 with the formation of the Birmingham, Erdington & Sutton Coldfield Railway Provisional Board in 1857, established by local busi-nessmen to make the 5 miles of railway to Sutton Coldfield. There was a dispute over the route to be followed, and two rival companies were set up, one proposing a line to the west of the Turnpike Road connecting to the LNWR at Aston, and one to the east connecting to the Midland Railway near Erdington Hall. In July 1859 a House of Commons Select Committee was appointed to determine which company's bill should receive the royal assent, but by then the Western company had

One of the first
trains on
the Sutton line at
Sutton Coldfield
station.

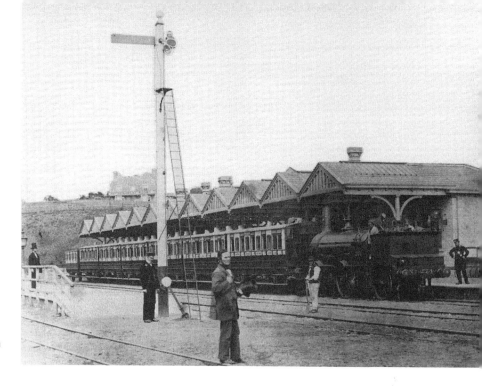

Plan of the
terminus station
in 1880. The
terminus was
demolished to
make way for a
through station in
1884.

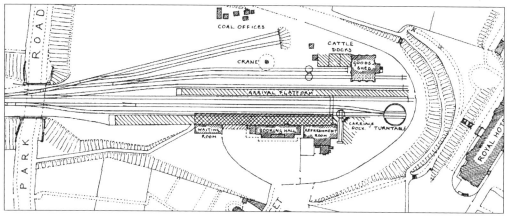

A luxury hotel, seen
here on a business card
of *c*. 1868, was built
above the terminus
station (now the
Council House).

TIME TABLES FOR FEBRUARY, 1870.

SUTTON COLDFIELD TO BIRMINGHAM.

UP	WEEK DAYS																		SUNDAYS			
	1 2 3	1 2 3	1 2 3	1 2 3	1 2 3	1 2 3 4	2 3	1 2 3	1 2 3	1 2 3	Gov	1 2 3	1 2 3	1 2 3	1 2 3	1 2 3	1 2 3	1 2 3	Gov	1 2 3
Sutton Coldfield	6 54	8 0	8 30	8 35	9 25	1045	1145	1240	2 20	2 30	2 55	5 0	5 50	6 45	8 25	1020	9 50	1 50	5 35	9 15
Wylde Green	6 54	8 3		8 39	9 29	1049	1149	1244		2 33	2 59	5 4	5 54	6 49	8 29	1024	9 54	1 54	5 38	9 19
Chester Road	6 57	8 7	8 35		9 32	1052	1152	1247	2 25	3 2	5 7	5 37	6 52	8 32	1027	9 57	1 57	5 41	9 22
Erdington	7 1	8 11		8 43	9 36	1056	1155	1251		2 37	3 5	5 11	6 1	6 56	8 77	1031	10 1	2 1	5 44	9 26
Gravelly Hill	7 4	8 14	8 40		9 39	1059	1158	1254	2 30	3 8	5 14	6 4	7 0	5 40	1035	10 4	2 4	5 47	9 29
Aston	7 8	8 18		8 49	9 43	11 3	12 2	1258	2 43	2 12	5 18	6 8	7 4	8 44	1039	10 8	2 8	5 51	9 33
Vauxhall				9 47		12 6				3 16	5 22	7 8		1012	2 12	5 55	9 37
Birmingham	7 20	8 30	8 54	9 0	9 55	1115	1215	1 10	2 43	2 53	3 26	5 35	6 20	7 18	8 55	1045	1020	2 20	6 5	9 47

BIRMINGHAM TO SUTTON COLDFIELD.

DOWN			Gov																	Gov			
	1 2 3	1 2 3	Gov	1 2 3	1 2 3	1 2 3	1 2 3	1 2 3	1 2 3	1 2 3	1 2 3	1 2 3	1 2 3	1 2 3	1 2 3	Gov	1 2 3	1 2 3	1 2 3
Birmingham	7 15	8 40	10 0	11 0	12 0	5 1	1 15	2 15	4 5	5 15	6 15	6 35	7 40	9 15	11 5		9 5	1 15	2 35	5 35
Vauxhall		8 45	10 8	11 5		2 31	4 10			7 45		9 10	1 20	2 43	5 40
Aston	7 22	8 49	1012	11 9	12 7	1 22	2 25	4 14	5 27	6 42	7 49	9 22	1112	9 14	1 24	2 47	5 44
Gravelly Hill	7 26	8 53	1016	1113	1211	1 15	2 29	4 18	5 26	6 25	7 53	9 26	1116	9 18	1 28	2 51	5 48
Erdington	7 29	8 56	1019	1116	1214	1 28	2 32	4 21	5 29	6 48	7 56	9 29	1119	9 21	1 31	2 54	5 51
Chester Road	7 33	9 0	1023	1119	1218	1 20	2 34	4 25	5 33	6 30	8 0	9 33	1123	9 25	1 35	2 58	5 55
Wylde Green	7 37	9 4	1027	1123	1222	1 32	2 44	4 39	5 37	6 52	8 4	9 37	1127	9 29	1 39	3 2	5 59
Sutton Coldfield	7 43	9 10	1033	1129	1228	1 28	1 38	2 49	4 35	4 36	6 38	6 58	8 10	9 43	1133	9 35	1 45	3 8	6 5

Railway timetable.

been taken over by the LNWR, and this settled the matter in favour of the line from Aston to Sutton to the west of the main road. This line was duly built, and opened on 4 June 1862.

It was a double-track line, but at first there was one passenger train operating a shuttle service between Sutton and Birmingham seven times a day. The engine was detached at the Sutton terminus station, turned on the turntable, and shunted past the train to be attached at the other end for the return journey. In the summer of 1862 a large number of excursion trains were run from Birmingham to Sutton, bringing crowds to Sutton Park, and the expectation was raised that Sutton would become a fashionable resort. However, the luxury hotel built above the terminus proved un-profitable. A plan of the station in 1880 (page 123) shows an extensive goods yard with coal merchants' offices as well as pens for cattle and sheep, showing that there was considerable goods traffic. The timetable for 1870 shows that the number of trains had increased to sixteen a day, with several trains to Birmingham in the morning rush hour and to Sutton in the evening. The line was already being used primarily for commuter traffic, and this has been its main function ever since.

The advent of the railway was seen by later Victorian writers as marking the end of 'old Sutton', a rural market town idyll suddenly broken into by the harsh industrial age. However, Sutton was changing before 1862, and the population had already increased by 50 per cent in the first half of the century. In 1859 new houses in Boldmere were described as belonging to 'clerks of £100 a year whose business is in Birmingham'. The rate of growth increased after 1861, with an extra 1,300 in 1871. By 1881 a further 1,800 brought the total up to 7,737, and ease of travel to Birmingham by rail was an important factor. The replacement of half a dozen horse-drawn omnibuses that took more than an hour over bumpy roads in 1860 by sixteen trains a day in 1870 that made the same journey in less than half the time smoothly and comfortably was a revolution.

In 1879 the Midland Railway opened its line through Sutton Park and Walmley, connecting its Black Country lines with its East Midland network at Water Orton. This was mainly a goods line for through traffic, but there were some passenger trains to Birmingham from the stations at Streetly, Sutton Park, Sutton Town and Penns. In 1884 the London & North Western Railway opened its extension of the Sutton branch to Lichfield, with a new and bigger station at Sutton with extra platforms and waiting rooms. On the same line, the station at Four Oaks had additional platforms and sidings in anticipation of heavy use on race days at Four Oaks Park.

The continuing increase in population brought demands for even better public transport, particularly after the successful introduction of trams in Birmingham and

A bus waits outside the Royal Oak Hotel at the top of Mill Street in 1925. (*Norman Evans Collection*)

The railway line cuts a swathe through Sutton Park.

elsewhere. The corporation applied for an act of Parliament to set up a tramway system in Sutton in 1902, but the application was not successful, largely because of the opposition of the London and North Western Railway Company, which argued that the tramway would duplicate its existing services. By that time the technology of road building had greatly advanced, and the Borough's Highways Committee was reporting progress on making and surfacing the town's roads at almost every council meeting. The improved roads made the cheap horse-drawn omnibuses a popular alternative to rail travel, and in 1913 the Birmingham & Midland Motor Omnibus Company ('Midland Red') introduced its first Sutton Coldfield service. Bus services steadily gained in popularity and were extended to serve all parts of the town, but it was not until 1938 that a by-law prohibiting double-decker buses in the town was lifted. Although private cars were becoming common in Sutton, most of the population was still heavily dependent on public transport and in 1937 the railway timetable listed forty-two trains to Birmingham every weekday.

In the second half of the twentieth century most goods were carried by road and the use of the private car became almost universal, leading to demands for the further expansion and improvement of the road network. The A38 Sutton by-pass was opened in 1973 and the ring road in the town centre in 1974, but a planned relief road to take traffic away from the High Street was shelved. Meanwhile the railway service saw changes, first with the replacement of steam engines by diesel power in 1956, then by electrification in 1993. The Sutton Park Line, which had stopped carrying regular passenger services, continued to be used by goods traffic.

TEN

Education, Religion and Social Life

U ntil 1824 the warden and society had to seek approval from the Court of Chancery for any big decisions. This was because the court was considering a charge brought against the warden and society by some inhabitants (William Twamley and others) who alleged that the corporation's funds were not being used to the best advantage. Both sides in the case wished to see the establishment of elementary education for all, but the details were disputed. In 1824 the court issued a final scheme 'for the application of the increased revenue', thirty-two years after the injunction limiting the corporation's activities had been imposed. During this period over £40,000 had accumulated in the funds, and the scheme provided for the bulk of this to be used for education. Three elementary schools were built, at Hill, Walmley and in the town centre, and a school of industry was established for older girls. It was expected that at least 240 children would attend the schools, and provision was made for a clothing allowance of £2 for boys and £1 11s 6d for girls each year. The schools opened in 1826 and by June 1827 the arrangements had been finalised. Permanent teachers were employed and all the places for pupils had been taken up. The syllabus was according to the principles of the National School, which provided for elementary education as well as the moral and religious instruction specified in the scheme. Children would leave the schools at the age of twelve, when boys could be put to apprentice at the corporation's expense if necessary. Girls could stay on at the school of industry, learning sewing, knitting, and spinning, making clothes for the schoolgirls and socks for the boys, and making up the linen for the charities.

The original Hill School at Mere Green, now a restaurant.

Detail of a sketch by Miss Bracken, 'Sutton from The Cup', showing the church before the nave roof was raised and the original Town School of 1826 (centre left).

The original
Walmley School
of 1826, now a
private house.

The scheme was not as successful as it should have been, according to a later writer, W.K. Riland Bedford:

The mass of the inhabitants, too, it must be said, did not look so much at the quality as the costliness of the education they were to obtain. A saving of ten shillings [the old 6d a week charge] appeared to the father a much larger concession than the opportunity of getting accomplishments for his boy, which would ensure a good start in life; while the farmers and their labourers regarded the schools, the one as a bonus to keep down wages, the other as an easy way of earning four suits of clothes at the expense of some gibberish their boy would forget as soon as he had worn out the last pair of inexpressibles. The scheme was quite good enough for popular opinion, and the tendency in administering it was to minimise its best provisions.

This was written by the rector, who had been closely involved from 1850 with the administration of the schools, and who had often seen his advice ignored. There may be some exaggeration here, and he was perhaps repeating family tradition. However, his main objection to the scheme, the lack of provision for secondary education, remained unresolved until the 1870s.

William Webb, the headmaster of Bishop Vesey's Grammar School, where many of the local children had been educated, died in 1817, having been headmaster for fifty-three years. The new headmaster, Charles Barker, discontinued the elementary education, and taught only Latin and Greek. He rarely had more than five pupils, and an investigation in 1833 showed that he had converted the schoolroom into a private dining room for his own use, and put the scholars in the former laundry. A petition was raised by the inhabitants of Sutton in January 1834 to the trustees, calling for a more general education to be offered, relevant to the needs of the town, as only two or three scholars were attending the school. The rector (William Riland Bedford, the father of W.K. Riland Bedford) commented that '330 children receive an excellent English Education free of expense' thanks to the town's elementary schools, and the Grammar School could perform a useful function in providing education for those who wished to remain at school after the age of twelve. The Corporation Upper School was making provision for twenty-four such children, but a joint arrangement with the grammar school should be considered. The trustees ignored these proposals and supported Barker, who had soon cut the number of scholars to one boy

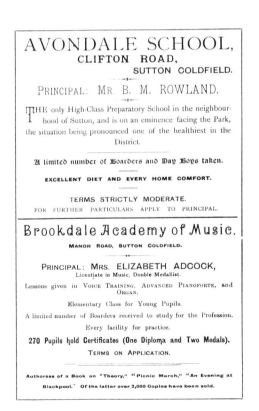

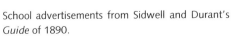

School advertisements from Sidwell and Durant's *Guide* of 1890.

The original St Joseph's School building, off Lichfield Road.

who sometimes attended. Barker suffered a fatal accident in 1842 and the new headmaster, together with new trustees, produced a new scheme for the education at the school, but it was not put into action. In 1853 there was an agreement with the corporation to admit twelve boys from the charity schools, but real expansion did not begin until the appointment of Joseph Wright as headmaster in 1859. The general education which was then offered attracted 26 students in 1863 and 69 in 1869, and by 1875 there were 105 on the roll.

As the population of Sutton increased new schools were opened at Wylde Green in 1840, at Boldmere in 1845 and at Walmley in 1850. By 1860 there were 600 children enrolled at the schools. For wealthier families there were a few private schools, and the number of such schools increased with the growth of population. Some of them attracted pupils from far afield, such as the preparatory school run by the Misses Cull at 69 Lichfield Road, where Francis Brett Young was a pupil in the 1890s.

The Education Act of 1870 set out to make universal education compulsory, and the administration of the schools passed to a School Board. Although the clergy were represented on the board, the emphasis was now firmly on instruction in the 'three Rs' – reading, writing and arithmetic. Religious and moral teaching, though still important, were less prominent. However, the teaching of religion was still of paramount importance in some quarters, and in Sutton denominational schools were proposed by Methodists, Congregationalists and Roman Catholics. The first Catholic school, St Joseph's, opened in 1878.

In the eighteenth century most Suttonians had been content to remain within the Church of England. Nevertheless there had been controversies. For example, in 1791 the curate, Mr Blick, preached a sermon that offended the new rector, John Riland. Blick said that conscience was a good guide to behaviour, but Riland maintained that the only guide was the revealed truth contained in the Bible. Blick was forced to go, but not before more than 1,500 copies of the offending sermon had been circulated. Another sermon preached in the parish church on the occasion of the death of King George III was also thought worthy of publication. It was preached on Sunday 27 February 1820 by the Revd Joseph Mendham, a local scholar. After six pages Mendham turns to the qualities of George III as a defender of the Protestant religion, and the remaining seven pages are a diatribe against Catholics and against any relaxation of the restrictions under which Catholics suffered: 'We owe it . . . to the true fortitude of our late Sovereign that the subjects and zealots of a foreign, a corrupt, an arrogant, and a sanguinary church, have not become part of the legislation of a Protestant country.'

The Roman Catholic church, 1834–1933, with the Priest's House behind, in Lichfield Road. The building is now occupied by offices.

The Catholic Emancipation Act of 1829 was followed in 1834 by the opening of the Catholic church (now the Guildhall) in Lichfield Road, just below Mendham's house, but his comments on this are not recorded. With the growth of the population more churches were needed, and after the establishment of churches at Hill (1835, consecrated by the Bishop of Worcester, hence Worcester Lane), Walmley (1845) and Boldmere (1857), Sutton parish was divided into four separate parishes centred on each church. By 1900 the Congregational church in Park Road (1879) and the Wesleyan Methodist church on The Parade (1888) were flourishing, together with iron churches at Maney and Whitehouse Common and a number of additional Nonconformist chapels.

Churches were also a focus for social life. The great Walmley Bazaar held in Sutton Park in 1841 to raise money for the new church was the talk of the town for many years after (see page 166). Great national events were celebrated in style. Sarah Holbeche was only a child at the time of the great Ox Roast on Ley Hill Common to celebrate the victory at Waterloo in 1815, but she could remember the cartloads of bread provided for the event going soggy in the rain. For the coronation of Queen Victoria in 1838 there was a dinner for 800 people laid out on twenty tables in Coleshill Street. Each person had a pound of meat (roasted sheep), at a total cost of £25, while £50 was spent on ale and £5 on tea. Some 200 quartern loaves (each weighing 4lb 6oz) were provided, and there was a band, fireworks and a ball in the

evening. These occasions were rare, however, and in most years the fairs and the
election of a new warden provided the main excitement. In January 1870 the newly
founded *Sutton Coldfield News* reported on an entertainment at the Town Hall given
by members of the congregation of the parish church, and there are also reports of
Christadelphian and Methodist events. The Town Hall housed a reading room where
there was a programme of penny readings, which were enjoyed by 'Olivia', who wrote
to the newspaper in 1870 complaining of the lack of public amusements in Sutton
Coldfield, and asking why a ball had not been arranged that year.

Another disappointed letter writer reported on the South Staffordshire hunt: 'we
had a wretched day's sport on Tuesday at Hams Hall. All the Hams coverts blank,
ditto Moxhull, ditto Mr. Horsfall's and ditto New Hall. We found a fox in Sutton

Crystal Palace, Sutton Coldfield.

**Large and small Parties, School Treats, Picnic Parties, etc.,
Catered for at the lowest possible Terms.
Accommodation for 1500 Persons under cover.   Estimates on application.
Apartments at reasonable terms.   Refreshments, Teas, Dinners, etc.**

K. A. EVANS   -   -   -   -   -   **Proprietor.**

Advert for the Crystal Palace in the 1890 *Guide*.

Park later in the afternoon, but the foot people headed him and mobbed him, and he was killed instantly.' The newspaper listed seven hunt meetings: Atherstone on 1 January, North Warwickshire Hounds on the 3rd, 4th, 6th and 7th and South Staffordshire on the 4th and 7th. The same paper reported that seventy-nine subscribers had resolved to revive the Sutton cricket club, but later in the year they may have regretted it. The Sutton eleven was all out for a paltry 26 against Handsworth, and in the same week Belgrave bowled them all out for 29. Other amusements to cheer 'Olivia' that year were a ball at the Royal Hotel in February and the reopening of the Royal Parade Grounds in Clifton Road on 14 May. These pleasure gardens, set up in 1868, were very successful, especially after the addition of the Crystal Palace in 1879.

By 1890 the weekly newspaper had changed its name to the *Sutton Coldfield and Erdington News and North Warwickshire Advertiser*, but still retained the same format. The bulk of the paper consisted of syndicated national news and features (including a column of excruciating 'jokes'), several pages of advertisements and a page of local

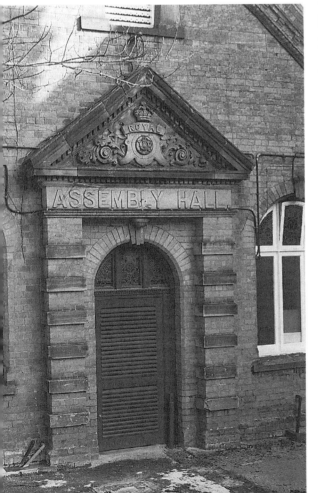

news. For entertain-ment, in the 4 January issue, there are accounts of the Institute Ball, the Mutual Improvement society gathering, the Fire Brigade's annual dinner and the Chrysanthemum Show. There was a two-day *Conversazione* at the Institute in the Town Hall, with 150 people attending each day. Football matches were now being reported – Boldmere St Michaels *v.* Old Veseyans at the Meadow Platt – and by April the last match of the season, Sutton Town v. Old Veseyans, was being billed as the big local derby. There was a lawn tennis club and a swimming club with 105 members as well as cricket matches to report, but the talk of the town was the

The Assembly Hall in King Edward Square, venue for the Institute Lectures in the 1890s.

The School of Art, Lichfield Road, built as a technical school in 1902.

series of Maypole Fêtes, where schoolchildren performed round a maypole on Holly Knoll in Sutton Park and took part in competitions. These were organised by the mayor, Benjamin Stone, and others interested in the late Victorian Gothic Revival of folklore and tradition, and were very popular, raising large sums for charity.

In 1870 there was a Museum of Natural History, later the Museum Public House on The Parade, and for more scientific-minded people a series of science classes was arranged in the Town Hall. Later in the century these were replaced by the Institute Lectures held in the Assembly Hall, and a more systematic education in science and technology was being offered in conjunction with Bishop Vesey's School. In 1900 the Borough Council decided to build a proper technical school and a competition for its design was advertised. The winning architect's design was chosen in 1902 and the firm of Crouch & Butler undertook the building of it. The new Technical School opened on Lichfield Road in September 1904 with 240 registered students. It grew in importance throughout the century under various titles, eventually becoming the present Sutton Coldfield College with its thousands of students and high academic achievements.

ELEVEN

Agriculture, Economy and Population Growth

The Enclosure Act of 1824 brought an extra 3,300 acres of common land into cultivation, nearly half as much as the existing farmland. This gave employment to many more agricultural workers, particularly during the time when new hedges were being planted, roads set out, drains laid, and the land cleared and improved for cultivation. When the railway engineer J.R. McLean reported in 1845 that Sutton was 'principally composed of an agricultural population' he was speaking the truth. In 1821, when the population was 3,450, there were 7,080 acres of farmland, and in 1851, when the population was 4,574, there were 10,400 acres, the increase in farmland being almost exactly in proportion to the population growth. Most of those engaged on the land were agricultural labourers. In 1826 the first Corporation School opened in Sutton. It had 39 pupils and the school log-book lists the parents' occupations: 19 were labourers, 6 worked in mills, 8 were tradesmen, 2 were professionals, 1 was a park-keeper and the others were widows.

In 1856 the ecclesiastical parish of Sutton Coldfield was divided. The new parishes – Walmley, Boldmere, Hill and Trinity (Sutton) – were used instead of the old quarters for some administrative purposes, such as collecting data for the 1861 census. This gave the population of Walmley as 621 and of Boldmere as 848. Boldmere, which extended from the park to Birmingham Road and as far north as Wyndley Lane (but excluding Maney) included a vast area of former common land. The 1861 census returns, which give the occupations of the householders, show that most people in Boldmere were employed in agriculture. There were three lodging houses owned by

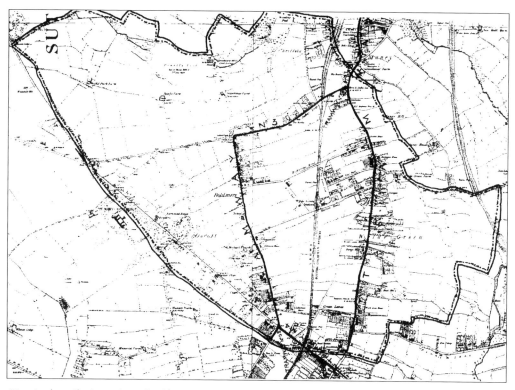

Map to show the boundary of Boldmere Parish as it was in 1861 and 1881. The base map was produced for the Sutton Coldfield Tramway Bill of 1902, and shows proposed tramways along Birmingham Road, Boldmere Road and Jockey Road. The Ordnance Survey map used for the bill was the first edition six-inch map of 1889, so most of the houses shown were there at the time of the 1881 census.

Irishmen describing themselves as agricultural labourers, where a further twenty-eight Irish agricultural labourers were lodgers, showing that migrant labour was still much in demand on the new farms. Of the other 163 households listed, 36 were headed by agricultural labourers. But Boldmere was not destined to remain agricultural for very long. The number of households there, 165 in 1861, had increased to 466 in 1881, and the population increased from 848 to 2,320, but by 1881 the Irish casual labourers had gone and only forty-one households were headed by agricultural labourers. Over these twenty years the population of Sutton had increased by just over 3,000. Nearly half of this increase was accounted for by Boldmere parish. The increase in Walmley over the same period was just nine households, from 137 to 146, with an increase in a population of 135, from 621 to 756.

This huge new population in Boldmere parish was principally due to the arrival of Birmingham businessmen who resided in Boldmere and commuted to their factories.

The Spade Mill in Stonehouse Road near Boldmere Gate in a drawing by Ken Williams from a 1910 photograph.

Their presence brought some new employment opportunities. For example, 44 of the households in 1881 were headed by gardeners compared with 7 in 1861, and 10 were coachmen. Many of the servants in the households of the newly wealthy were also recruited locally. Although the spade mill at Powells Pool was still working in 1881, it employed far fewer workers than the 65 men, 69 boys and 4 women recorded in 1861, and was now rolling steel for the steel pen manufacturers of Birmingham. Walmley parish had suffered a more disastrous decline in local employment in 1859 when the wire mill at Penns closed down as the business was transferred to Hay Mills near Yardley. Penns Mill was a flourishing factory, and had it remained in production for another ten years, when the company Webster & Horsfall was manufacturing wire for the telegraph cable beneath the Atlantic to America, this part of Sutton may have become a manufacturing district instead of reverting to rural peacefulness.

Walmley parish included the part of Sutton between Kingsbury Road and the River Tame. This area was chosen by the Tame & Rea Drainage Board as the site of its sewage works at the end of the nineteenth century, an undertaking that expanded to cover the whole area in the early twentieth century, served by its own light railway. The E brook flowed through Minworth to the Tame, feeding the pools serving Plants Forge, once another part of the Webster & Horsfall business; a boundary change added this area to Sutton Coldfield in 1929. On the E brook above Penns was New Hall Mill, which in 1861 was at the height of its importance, catering for the increased demand for flour to feed the population of the growing towns. It had four millers keeping the four sets of stones grinding all through the night at busy times. In 1861 the mill machinery was renewed with the latest improved modifications, and the mill was advertised in 1882 as 'To let near two lines of railways, water corn mills, two wheels, driving two pairs each. All necessary machinery, including silks and exhaust'. By 1882, though, the local mills were in decline, unable to compete with the big flour mills at the ports.

The eastern side of Sutton saw the creation or expansion of several estates after the commons were enclosed, with Bagot of Pype Hayes extending his estate over Eachelhurst, the Penns Estate expanding to include over 500 acres, and the New Hall Estate of the Chadwicks and the Moxhull Estate of the Hackets being consolidated. New estates at Falcon Lodge and Fox Hill were created as country residences for wealthy townsmen, partly by the purchase of common land which was sold to cover the cost of enclosure. Fox Hill was built for John Valentine, a musician who dabbled in the arts. He

Fox Hill House.

Bottle kiln at Fox Hill.

set up a decorative tile works there but soon became bankrupt, and the bottle kiln which can still be seen beside its flooded claypit was never used again. Further north the Canwell Estate of Lord Wenlock was extended into Sutton, characterised by smallholdings formed by the rationalisation of a patchwork of squatters' holdings and newly enclosed commons.

Hill parish, to the north of Sutton, was also late to lose its rural character. In 1861 the census showed that 80 of the 119 households in the Little Sutton area were headed by farmers or farmworkers, while 51 of the 95 households in the Hill Village neighbourhood were engaged in agriculture. This had been an area of small farms and cottages before enclosure, with many of the squatters and cottagers relying partly on the extensive commons to make a living. Many of them worked as agricultural labourers after enclosure, but a significant number were able to make a living from cottage industries. Thirty-three households were headed

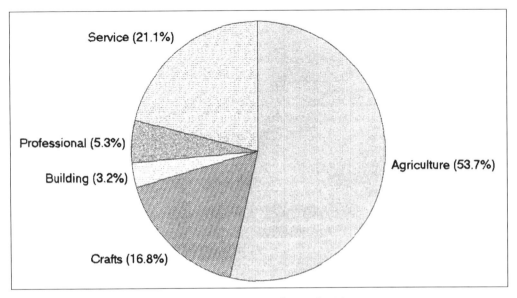

Occupations of heads of households in Hill, Mere Green and Ley Hill, 1861.

by craftsmen or artisans, such as carpenters, blacksmiths and wheelwrights. The area had changed little by 1881, with only nine additional houses, giving a total of 238 houses and a population of 997. The rest of Hill parish, to the west of Lichfield Road, comprising Four Oaks and Hill Hook, was equally rural. Although the number of houses had almost doubled between 1821 and 1861 as the commons were enclosed, in the twenty years from 1861 to 1881 the increase was only five households and sixty-nine people, giving a total population of 363 living in 91 households.

The growth in population in Trinity parish, which included the town centre, was mainly on the west side of Birmingham Road, and was largely due to the influx of prosperous businessmen who would commute to Birmingham. In this part of the town the population more than doubled between 1861 and 1881, from 511 to 1,295. On the other side of the road growth was less spectacular, from 1,457 to 2,006, and was made up more of the natural growth of the existing population and of people in the service sector than of commuters. It was on this eastern side of Sutton that some less pleasant works were sited – leather-curing near South Parade, gun-barrel grinding near Holland Road and in 1853 the gas works on the corner of Coleshill Road and Riland Road. The works was supplying gas to houses and street lights in most of the centre of Sutton by 1870 (the first gas lamp, set up on The Dam in 1861, is shown in on page 112; see also page 142). However the plant and equipment soon became obsolete and the works closed in 1892; the whole of Sutton Coldfield was then supplied with Birmingham Corporation gas. The increased population gave rise to an increase in commerce, and by 1880 the first new shops had been opened on the newly christened Parade (formerly known as 'The Dam'). There were already a number of shops nearby, but the development of The Parade shops over the next twenty years established the division of the town centre into a business quarter in High Street and a commercial quarter on The Parade which still holds good.

Over the next twenty years (1881–1901) the population of Sutton grew from 7,737 to 14,264, a rise that was almost entirely due to the influx of people coming to live in Sutton but working elsewhere. Although many of the newcomers were well-off, the working-class population was also growing. As James Speight recalled:

Come with me to the Parade, early, about six o'clock, and men are hurrying to the station. They are catching the 6.15. They are the workmen, the manual labourers, they wear cloth caps. In an hour's time, come to the Parade again,

High Street in 1925, showing the ornate electric lamp at the top of Mill Street and the plain gas one on the corner of Coleshill Street.

The Parade looking south, in a drawing by Ken Williams from a 1960s photograph.

Parade shops, *c.* 1910.

Detail of above – the shop with the pictures on show is W.H. Smith's, next door to Harpur's dress shop.

and men are hurrying to the station again, they are catching the 7.30. They are the clerks, the office workers, and the shop assistants. They wear bowler hats. Come once more to the Parade with me, about nine-fifteen. Here they come, the top-notchers, the bosses, the stock-brokers, the bank managers and lawyers; there's a smell of cigars. They do not hurry. They are going by the 9.30 non-stop. They wear black silk top hats. And as they pass Park Road and turn into Station Street, and a breeze flutters their frock coats, we will say good-bye to the ghosts of 1902.

In 1912, when the population of Sutton exceeded 20,000, the *Kelly's Directory* for Sutton listed over 500 commercial undertakings, almost all of them shops, farms, public houses or professional services. The larger concerns included two laundries in the Coleshill Street area; Lloyds' brickworks at Wheatmore; Powells Pool Ltd, steel rollers; Robinson's timber merchants at Wyndley Pool; Read & Sons' mineral water factory on the corner of Holland Road and Lower Queen Street; the Four Oaks Spraying Machine Co. in Belwell Lane, Four Oaks; and the Yote Factory, makers of small components in brass and steel, in Mere Green Road. The *Directory* listed Boldmere, Wylde Green, New Oscott and Walmley separately, and all 150 commercial entries for these districts were providers of goods or services to the residential population. The *Directory* shows many farms still working, and there was still a livestock market in Sutton (held in Anchorage Road at the rear of the Royal Hotel). There was a Saturday open-air market held in the space between The Parade and Lower Parade, but these markets all ceased to function in the 1920s.

In the ten years between 1891 and 1901 the population of Sutton increased by 6,000, and a further 6,000 over the next ten years gave a total population in 1911 of 20,132. The next decade saw a growth of only 3,000, but a further 6,900 boosted the number recorded in the 1931 census to 29,928. An even more rapid rate of expansion followed as large estates and farms were developed for housing, and the population figures for the next two censuses were 47,590 in 1951 and 72,143 in 1961. Demand for new housing continued at a high level for the rest of the century, the population having risen to over 90,000 by the year 2000. Plans for the development of the town had been produced in 1926 and at later times, culminating in Birmingham City Council's Unitary Development Plan in 1991. This designated those areas that were reserved for housing, public open space, green belt, industry and other uses, and it preserves the features of Sutton Coldfield as they were at the end of the twentieth century.

TWELVE

Housing and Health

In 1822 the warden and society identified a site for the proposed new school in Sutton near the bottom of Mill Street. Although the land belonged to the corporation, five cottages would have to be demolished to make way for the school, so the tenants of the cottages were duly approached and asked to give up their tenancies. Some of them were reluctant to move out and the negotiations dragged on until 1825, when all five were found alternative accommodation, some in the new almshouses in Mill Street. This was an early example of good housing management on the part of the warden and society. Planning for new developments which involved the demolition of existing houses, was already familiar in that part of Sutton, where the act of Parliament of 1807, which established the Turnpike trust, authorised works at Mill Street. The trust was given power to widen and straighten the road, and 'to take down such part of a certain Messuage Cottage, or Tenement and Pig Stye, and to take the land on which such part of the said Buildings are erected and also to take so much of the land occupied therewith as shall be necessary, the whole of which belong to the warden and society, and are now in the occupation of Richard Granger'. Most of the cottages in Sutton had been built on common land at some time in the past, and were usually regarded as belonging to the warden and society.

The Enclosure Award regularised this ownership and gave the warden and society full title. From 1826 the old *laissez-faire* attitude to the cottages, where assistance was given as need arose, was replaced by a more determined policy of making sure that the cottages were kept in good repair, or even completely rebuilding some of them. On 9 June 1830 the corporation decided

The site of the Town School in a sketch dating from the eighteenth century, showing some of the cottages which were to be demolished.

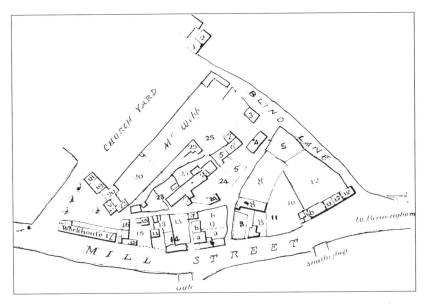

Plan of Mill Street from the 1811 Corporation Survey. The Turnpike Road improvements took part of no. 11 (Joseph James's garden), 9b (Thomas Norris's pig-sty), part of 9a (a building belonging to John Farmer), no. 14 (Richard Granger's house) and the garden wall of the workhouse. The Town School took the properties numbered 8 (Widow Yates's house, shoemaker's shop and three gardens), 10 (Widow Wilkins' house and garden), 11 (Joseph James's house and garden) and 12 and 13 (James Bonehill's and John Heath's houses and garden).

Pickerill's cottage.

that the cottage at Four Oaks occupied by Pickerill be rebuilt on a new scite [*sic*] in front of the old one. That Mr Solomon Smith do the carpenters work and superintend the whole provided he sends in his accounts to the present time within a week after he hath notice thereof. That John Pratt do the brickwork and that W. Brown do the glazing and each to make separate accounts.

This new cottage, now 1 Walsall Road, situated in the sharp angle between Streetly Lane and Walsall Road, replaced

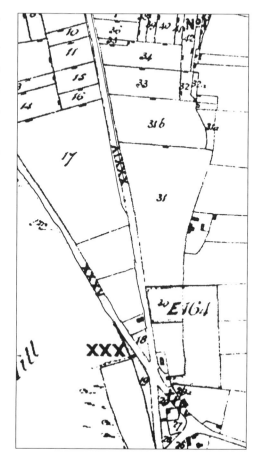

Detail of the Four Oaks section of the Enclosure Award map. Road XXXV is Streetly Lane, while XXXIV is Walsall Road. The small triangular plot 18 was awarded to the warden and society, and Pickerill's cottage was rebuilt on this ⅛-acre site; the map shows his previous dwelling in the ¼-acre field next to it. Only the fields that were previously common land are numbered.

one which was not only in poor condition but also inconveniently sited, isolating the triangle of newly enclosed land from the neighbouring fields. The old cottages, constructed of flimsy timber frames infilled with wattle and daub, with threadbare thatch overhanging the low walls, were gradually replaced with brick and tile houses, or in some cases demolished altogether. Some may have been built of cob, a mixture of marl and straw. George Eliot writes of 'the grey-thatched roof of the mud cottage' on the common at Hayslope, a fictional place somewhere in East Warwickshire, not far away. The cottages are included in a survey of corporation property of about 1811, where each property is assigned a yearly value. Pickerill's house was then worth £2 10s, whereas Widow Scott's house (next to the Four Oaks entrance to Sutton Park, now 47 Four Oaks Road) was worth £5 5s.

Some cottages were privately owned. For example, the four tenements and gardens at Four Oaks on the corner of Park Drive were rented out to agricultural labourers by William Farnell. Another early example of speculative building was the terrace of six houses built by Mr Hayward on Lower Parade, then known as The Dam. Most of the cottages were on public land, however, probably the result of squatting over several centuries, as had occurred in many other parts of the country: 'Some of the ancients still occupied cottages on land which had been ceded to their fathers as "squatters' rights", and probably all the small plots on which the houses stood had originally been so ceded.' (Flora Thompson, *Lark Rise to Candleford*) The process was still continuing at the beginning of the nineteenth century, as shown by the appearance at Four Oaks of Nanny Fisher's cottage in the 1824 Corn Rent schedule but not recorded in 1811 (this appears to have been a tiny shack, and was demolished when she died). No doubt many of these tumbledown houses were short-lived. Cottages were to be found in all parts of Sutton, with particularly low-value ones on Reddicap Hill, where Widow Bird's cottage had an annual value of only £1, at Bulls Lane and at Hill Wood, where Pratt's house was valued equal with Widow Bird's at £1. The greatest concentration of cottages and houses on warden and society land was between Mill Street and Trinity Hill in the town centre. Here there were twenty houses; several of them were very small, occupying only 1 perch (30 square yards) of land, but those to be demolished to make way for the school were of slightly higher value. Joseph James's cottage at £2 10s was the lowest, while Widow Yates had a house, a shoemaker's shop and three gardens worth £7 10s – and it was the widow who objected most strongly to being evicted.

At the other end of the scale, some of the big houses were in decline. Langley Hall had come into the possession of Sir Robert Peel but was in poor condition and was

Fairview Cottages, Bulls Lane, built for farm workers in the eighteenth century.

demolished in 1822. The Chadwick family hardly ever visited New Hall, and Marlpit Hall was converted to workmen's tenements. Moor Hall, Four Oaks Hall and the newly improved Ashfurlong Hall were flourishing, however, and the big houses built at 'the top of Sutton' in the eighteenth century – Moat House, The Rookery and The Anchorage – housed the top gentry. Many of the houses in High Street belonged to the local squirarchy – the Jesson, Hacket, Holt, Chadwick and Addis Estates

Wigginshill Cottages, typical late Victorian housing for farmworkers.

The Georgian stone façade of Ashfurlong Hall. The new front was built from locally quarried stone for Mr Vaughton at the end of the eighteenth century.

The rear of Ashfurlong Hall, an extended stone farmhouse of the sixteenth century.

Old Bank Place, four cottages behind 24 High Street.

all included a High Street house – and the substantial Georgian façades which can still be seen are a reminder of the importance of outward show in that age of patronage. In the nineteenth century the households of gentry and professional men predominated in High Street, interspersed with shops and public houses.

By the early nineteenth century, in many of the plots behind the High Street houses, outbuildings had been converted into dwellings, or rebuilt as houses to be occupied by artisans, servants and labourers. Some of these can still be seen, for example at Old Bank Place. On the other side of High Street, in Whitehouse's Court (demolished to make way for King Edward Square) there were seven households in 1851. The census records show that one was headed by a journeyman spademaker who had seven children. The rest were the households of labourers, most of them originally from Ireland, and included eight lodgers, seven of them Irish labourers. In all there were forty-two inhabitants of Whitehouse's Court. This process of converting outbuildings into dwelling houses probably met most of the housing needs of the growing population up to 1850, and had a long history – the will of Thomas Clifton, who lived next to the Three Tuns, refers to the new house he had built next door in 1684. The will of Abraham Outon in 1771 refers to two new houses. He lived in a farmhouse in Coleshill Street (now Vesey Gardens), and the new houses replaced former farm buildings; the farmhouse was later converted into a public house called The Old Sun.

Elsewhere in Sutton new houses were needed to accommodate the farmers and farm labourers working the newly enclosed lands. On the north-west side of Sutton the Canwell estate of Lord Wenlock had obtained considerable property, and the houses built by the Estate for smallholders and farm workers in a characteristic style can still be seen, for example in Slade Lane and Weeford Road. (The Canwell Estate was later purchased by Birmingham Corporation. More small-holdings were set out, with houses of a distinctive style, after the First World War as part of a national movement to provide 'homes fit for heroes'.) In the 1830s new farms were built in Streetly Lane and Walsall Road on the former Four Oaks Common. The number of houses at Four Oaks in 1856 was thirty-nine compared with twenty-two in 1824, before enclosure, but hardly any more houses were built there in the next thirty years. A small cluster of dwellings grew up on the former common at the top of Four Oaks Common Road, including the original Crown Inn. There were other such groups of new houses elsewhere on the former commons, for example at Slade Road, on the Whitehouse Triangle and on Reddicap Heath, but none of these became a new

Slade Farm, a nineteenth-century Canwell Estate house.

centre of settlement on the scale of Walmley and Boldmere. The present centre of Walmley Village had been open common, and the road pattern was laid out by the enclosure commissioner in such a way that it attracted new development. It suffered an early blow with the closure of Penns wire mill in 1860, and hardly grew at all until the twentieth century, whereas Boldmere village centre, which also grew up at the junction of enclosure roads, enjoyed steady growth. At first most of the housing was working

Hill Crest, Worcester Lane, a twentieth-century Canwell Estate house.

class, for farmworkers, spade-mill workers, artisans and servants, but as mentioned above this area was the first part of Sutton to attract new housing of a different kind, the 'villa residences' of newly wealthy industrialists from the neighbouring manufacturing towns. Before enclosure building development on the commons had been unattractive because of the impossibility of establishing legal title to the property, but after enclosure the land was privately owned and houses could safely be built on the former commons.

The villa residences were mainly along Chester Road and Birmingham Road. These were large houses with impressive drawing rooms and dining rooms and accommodation for several servants as well as for the family; most of them occupyied 2 or 3 acres of ground. One such was Marchmount House in Birmingham Road, built in 1853 for Henry Fielding, a Birmingham silversmith, on a site of 3½ acres; Marchmount, like many others, has since been demolished to make way for new housing developments. The land was being viewed with an eye to its potential for building. Emmanuel College, Cambridge, owned property in Sutton which was

Rear view of Marchmount House in 1895, viewed from the extensive pleasure grounds. (*Wilkinson Papers*)

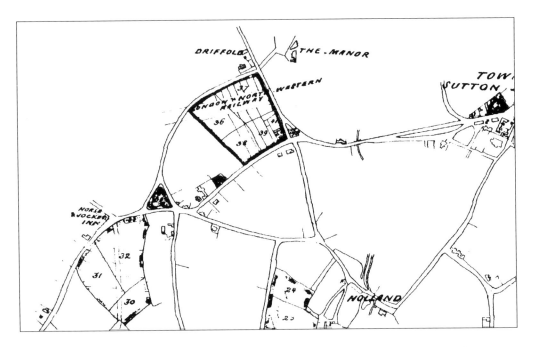

Part of a sketch plan of the Emmanuel College lands in Sutton Coldfield made in 1865 by Charles Cooper. He suggested fields numbered 30–2 (near Pilkington Avenue) and 36–41 (off Maney Hill) as possible sites for development.

let out on 21-year leases, and these were due for renewal in 1865. The college's surveyor in Sutton, Charles Cooper, reported on 'those portions of the estate which are likely to become building properties during the next term of years'. One site, fronting Birmingham Road between Manor Hill and Bishops Road, 'may be divided into lots of about an acre with frontages thereto and should be for buildings of from £250 to £300 value', while another (now Pilkington Avenue) was 'situated upon a beautiful elevation commanding extensive views of the surrounding district'. He ends his report with the warning that 'there is a very great quantity of land now offered to be let on building leases in the Parish'. In the event the Emmanuel College property was not developed until the twentieth century.

During the Railway Bill Enquiry of 1859 land to the east of Gravelly Hill in Erdington was described as 'beautiful sites for building' and 'calculated for villa residences', while to the west the land was 'more adapted to one or two acre plots and not so large a class of house'. In 1859 the rector said at the enquiry that the population of Boldmere had gone from zero to over a thousand souls in the last twenty years, many of them being clerks and small business men who lived in houses not so good as the villa residences, and their place of work was in Birmingham. More modest houses of this type were also being built near the centre of Sutton, as Sarah Holbeche observed in her diary: '1846 – Mr Sadler's field at Maney cut up into building plots; 1860 – Duke Street named; 1864 – Tudor Hill and Lodge begun.'

The Tudor Hill estate had been transferred to the warden and society as part of the 'Hartopp Exchange', when Sir Edmund Hartopp of Four Oaks Hall had been allowed to take in 63 acres of Sutton Park, giving up 93 acres in exchange. Some 51 acres of this land was added to Sutton Park, the income from the remaining 42 acres (the Tudor Hill Estate) being used to augment the charitable income of the warden and society. All this had been settled in 1827, but it was only in 1864 that the demand for high-status housing in Sutton warranted the development of the estate for building. The nearby Anchorage Estate was laid out and advertised in July 1870 for sale in twenty-six building lots, the owner being R.H. Sadler, whose Duke Street property had already been divided into building plots in 1846. Conditions were imposed to prevent the Anchorage Estate from being inappropriately developed: 'No Dwelling House shall be of less cost and value, exclusive of outbuildings, than £500.

Drumcrieff House in Tudor Hill, 1901. (*Wilkinson Collection*)

No manufacture nor any noxious, dangerous, or offensive process shall be carried out on any lot sold.' After the first four houses were built, there was a delay of sixteen years before development resumed, during which time the Midland Railway built its Sutton Park Line. Anchorage Road was already in existence and the railway was obliged to provide a bridge. The same foresight had been shown in 1858, when John Smith, the owner of Wylde Green Farm, laid out Highbridge Road and Station Road so that when the railway came in 1862 it had to provide bridges.

Richard Sadler developed another part of the Anchorage Estate fronting Lichfield Road more intensively, with a terrace of ten houses known as Wellington Terrace. When Tudor Road was laid out in 1892, the intention was to build twenty-two houses, and these had been completed by 1899. The houses were for rent, but the original builder and owner, Roger Harley, mortgaged most of them in order to raise capital to develop Lyndon Road and Park Road. Lyndon Road has twenty-six houses each side and Park Road twenty-five, although both are shorter than Tudor Road. At Reddicap Hill development was more piecemeal. Charles Adams built a house and shop in 1884, four houses in 1889, four in 1891, three in 1893, four in 1894, two in 1896, two in 1898, four in 1899, two in 1900 and four in 1903, as his cash flow allowed, bearing in mind the availability of plots of land and the state of the housing market. Many of his buildings were of poor quality, 'two-up and two-down' houses fronting directly on to the street. Some have since been demolished. In contrast, many of the houses on the more prestigious estates were designed by notable architects and were built to a high standard. Most of the buildings in Sutton listed as being of architectural interest date from this time, notably by Arts and Crafts architects such as Bidlake, Bateman, Crouch, Butler and Titley. The Four Oaks Park Estate, Anchorage Road and the Tudor Road Estate are all included in Conservation Areas. From 1886 the Borough of Sutton Coldfield had been the planning authority, with a duty to see that the new developments had proper foundations, damp courses, drains and sewers. The building plans submitted for all the new houses survive, and show that the early pattern of small developments of one or two houses for a private owner gradually gave way in the twentieth century to the development of larger estates of houses built by specialist firms, as building for rent gave way to building for sale. Local authority housing for rent was also built, particularly between 1920 and 1970, at first on a small scale at Tower Road, Cofield Road and Ebrook Road, but later on a larger scale at Falcon Lodge and Hill West.

Right: Map of the Tudor Road Conservation Area, showing the lower density of housing in Tudor Road.

Middle: Lyndon Road.

Bottom: Tudor Road.

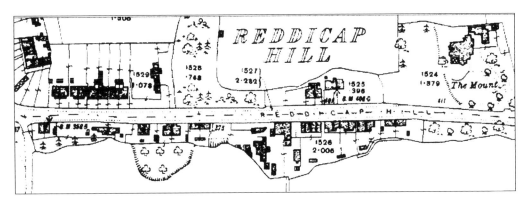

Reddicap Hill – Charles Adams' houses are mostly on the south side.

Reddicap Hill, the houses fronting directly on to the narrow pavement. (*Janet Jordan*)

Woodgate in Hartopp Road, built by W.H. Bidlake for himself in 1896.

The imposing entrance to The Leasowes in Lichfield Road, designed by Ernest Newton in 1893.

Stone building on Reddicap Hill, once a dwelling house.

Writing in the 1890s, Richard Holbeche bemoaned the passing of 'Old Sutton', with its characterful cottages and colourful figures. One of the main reasons for the change was the desire to have a more healthy environment, and the reports of the Medical Officer of Health show that this was being achieved by the provision of proper drains and dry houses with good water supplies. In the 1920s the council was required to maintain a list of unfit housing, which led to the demolition of some of the more picturesque but unhealthy cottages (see above right). When illness did strike, those who could not afford the doctor's fees and medicines were in trouble, and were obliged to fall back on charities to help out. If they were able they would subscribe to the Provident Dispensary which stood on the corner of Rectory Road and Coleshill Street, enabling them to receive proper treatment. In 1891 the District Nursing Home was set up on Birmingham Road, and in 1907 the Cottage Hospital was established in the same building, extended in 1911 and again later. The Cottage Hospital could

Oakhurst.

not develop further on its existing site, so in 1943 a house called Good Hope was
purchased to accommodate overflow convalescent patients. The site was expanded in
the 1950s to cater for additional patients from the General Hospital in Birmingham,
and soon developed into the Good Hope Hospital of today. Meanwhile, an even
grander house, Oakhurst in Anchorage Road, was converted into a maternity unit
with fourteen beds in four wards. It opened on 1 July 1946 and closed when the
new maternity wards at Good Hope were built in 1967.

The good health enjoyed by the townsfolk had often been attributed to the
bracing Coldfield air. Miss Bracken wrote of the crowds coming to Sutton in
the 1850s: 'multitudes imported for a few hours respiration of Coldfield air.
Long may it be worth the seeking', while two centuries earlier Robert Burton
had commended the air of Sutton in his *Anatomy of Melancholy*, published in
1621. Sunshine and fresh air were the main elements in the treatment of patients
suffering from pulmonary consumption at Dr Bodington's sanatorium in Maney.
George Bodington was the first to recommend dry frosty air for this condition, in
his *Essay on the treatment and cure of pulmonary consumption* published in 1840,
based on his observations at Sutton. As well as his sanatorium, which stood on
Maney Corner, he ran an asylum for lunatics at Driffold House. At the end of
the nineteenth century the former Royal Hotel was converted into a sanatorium,

Advertisement for the Royal Hotel in 1890, shortly before it was converted into a sanatorium.

taking advantage of its airy situation, but it was not a success and the building became the Borough Council House in 1902. It was not only the air which was worth the seeking, as Sutton's water was also highly prized. Rowton's Well in Sutton Park was believed to have healing powers, as Twamley noted in his history:

Admission details from the Sanatorium Prospectus.

On the SW side of the Park, is another bathing-place, called Rowton Well, which has been a noted Well, for a great number of years; For scorbutic eruptions etc. Very much resorted to by the working mechanics of Walsall, West Bromwich, and that neighbourhood. Indeed all round about that smoky country, to bathe in its pure waters.

Illustration from Horton's poem 'Sutton Park', 1850.

THIRTEEN
Sutton Park

S utton Park had a recreational origin. It began in the twelfth century as a deer
park where the lord of the manor would come hunting, but by the fifteenth
century it was being exploited more for its timber and grazing. Bishop Vesey
confirmed this economic use of the park; he fenced the woods and stocked the park
with horses and cattle, to the great benefit of the poor and of the Corporation. The
charter of 1528, which gave the warden and society responsibility for the park, also
gave the inhabitants some rights to hunt small game, and this was a valued privilege.
By 1800 the park was beginning to be appreciated for its natural beauty. The
sculptor William Frederick Woodington recalled his childhood wanderings there:

> Many a time in half-holiday have I wandered in these woods; miles of
> heather and gorse surrounded me, and beautiful clear streams wandering
> through the wilds, the silver birch rising gracefully on every side, and where
> the streams were occasionally dammed up they formed lakes, reflecting the
> beauteous woods and all the varieties of light and shade, with now and then
> a long thin line of silver, the gentle air across the glassy surface, as beautiful
> as anything I have seen in the Cumberland lakes. These lessons nature to
> a child taught. However, things altered. I was carried to London, 1815, at
> nine years of age.

There were some attempts to improve and beautify the landscape of the park in about
1800, in the manner of the age. A glade was cut through Hollyhurst, partly to give
better access to grazing cattle, but also to give a distant prospect of the town, framed
by the woods on either side. Some rustic bridges were built, the brook in Blackroot
Valley was artificially tamed and in the Park House grounds an ornamental walk was

Engraving by Miss Bracken in the picturesque style, showing a party of sportsmen in the park with their guns and dogs. Her signature (a frond of bracken) and the date, 1854, are at the bottom left.

laid out. Otherwise the park was managed to give a good yield of timber and to provide grazing for cattle; several drainage schemes were carried out in the marshy areas to improve grazing. This regime resulted in the preservation of the woods, heaths and marshlands which give the park the appearance it has had for 2,000 years or more, with the addition of the man-made pools. A more positive approach to the management of the park was called for in response to the increasing demands made on it by the growing population. In 1853 a notice was posted by the warden and society prohibiting the pursuit of game in the park on the grounds that unrestricted hunting had almost destroyed all the game, and over-eager sportsmen were damaging the woods and fences in pursuit of it.

'The dissatisfaction originated with some regulations for sporting and other amenities of the Park, which caused certain opponents to form themselves into a "Park Protection society", meeting at the Green Man Inn, Erdington,' wrote Riland Bedford. One complaint about the corporation quickly led to others, and before long the government was petitioned for a new municipal charter after a mass meeting on Clifton's Hill attended by some 2,000 people. The resulting enquiry, held at Sutton in August 1855, had a negative outcome, but the statements of the witnesses about the park show how it was regarded at the time. Henry Fielding, a silverware manufacturer from Birmingham who had moved into his new house, 'Marchmount', at Wylde Green in 1853, said that the park was for poor inhabitants, to send their cattle into it; it had pasturage for horses and cattle, but not sheep. Mr Buggins who farmed Booth's Farm, south of Powells Pool, one of the farms established on park land under the clause of the 1528 charter; agreed: 'Cows, horses, asses and mules, any thing except sheep.' He also said that the value of the pasturage could be doubled by putting it 'through a run of cropping'. Mr Hayward, a timber merchant of Wyndley Mill, said the woods were not properly managed; he would replace all the oak woods with larch. Mr Parkes, spademaker at Stone House Forge (Powell's Pool), who employed thirty men, complained about the state of the roads, but also said 'Sutton Coldfield water is the best in England. There is nothing equal to it for hardening and tempering steel.' His idea for improving the park was to divide it into allotments: 'If a labourer had half-an-acre allotted to him, the first year in manure and labour it would probably cost him £10; at the average value of potatoes, it would produce him £15.' Mr George Jones, a Birmingham manufacturer who had lived in Sutton for five years, asserted: 'I could go into the Park and have nine brace of birds [wildfowl] and snipe besides.' Another Birmingham manufacturer, Edwin Lewis, who lived at Chester Road, said 'I bought my house at £2,000 because I thought we had a right to the Park.' The deputy steward, Mr Holbeche, explained that the poor got most benefit from the park, depasturing a horse or mule for 3s 4d and a cow for 20d, as well as cutting gorse and ling, and gathering fern for firing; improving the pasture would only benefit the relatively well-off. In his summing-up, the barrister speaking for the corporation, Mr Huddleston, said,

> What was their advice? 'The Pasture is wretched; we have a fine new scheme for Sutton Coldfield – crop the Park with carrots, turnips and potatoes.' This was the most unfortunate thing that ever emanated from the minds of the Birmingham gentlemen who seek this innovation; they have found out their mistake, for a more unpalatable suggestion to the inhabitants of Sutton Coldfield could not have been propounded . . . they did not want cupidity to deprive . . . those who enjoy the beauties of the Park of their pleasure.

Meanwhile, the beauties of the park were providing inspiration for Miss Bracken's fine series of engravings in the picturesque style, and for Mr Horton's poetry. In his poem 'Sutton Park' he rejoices in the solitude where no railway sounds intrude: 'Thy sacred haunts no railway change have found.' This solitude had recently been

In Sutton Park woods, by Miss Bracken.

Emblem of worth, within thy circling nook,
The chrystal gleams with unpretending look,
On heaven's high arch it keeps its glassy eye
And in its breast reflects the answering sky ;
Ethereal lustre o'er its surface glows,
And still more clear the pebbly depths disclose
Long may thy virtues to the poor bring health
(An ample balance for the want of wealth;)
Long may thy watery charm relief extend,—
Best of Physicians, and the poor man's friend
E'en now I love to seek thy wholesome spell
And plunge within the far-famed Rowton well

II.

In Nuthurst's windings would you stray,
Or o'er wild heath and length'ning way
　That leads to Rowton Well ?
Pellucid fount ! What annual scores
Thy stream to cleanliness restores
　The scribbled post may tell !
How many Smiths and Joneses came,
And left to thee their votive name,
How many more had done the same,
　Only they could not spell !

Poetry inspired by Sutton Park; (left) a stanza from Charles Barker's 'Guide to the Sutton Park Bazaar', 1841, and an extract from Horton's 'Sutton Park', 1850.

threatened by just such an intrusion. In August 1853 the warden and society had received a letter from the Mayor of Birmingham, H. Hawkes, requesting that they join with Birmingham and the Midland Railway in a project to build a 'crystal palace' in Sutton Park and make a line of railway from the Midland line at Bromford to terminate at or near the park. The object was stated to be to provide a place of recreation for the inhabitants of Birmingham, and the idea was enthusiastically supported by the Birmingham newspapers. The debate on the subject at a meeting of the Birmingham Town Council was fully reported in *Aris's Birmingham Gazette* on Monday 1 August 1853, in particular a speech by Alderman Cutler. He referred to the quantity of vehicles setting off from Birmingham with parties intent on enjoying a day out: 'He was credibly informed that not fewer than fifty "gipsy parties" left Birmingham in different ways on the previous day.' Other observers were commenting on the numbers flocking to the park:

And from Birmingham, the park is a place of great resort in the Summer-time of the year; by Gypsying-parties, who bring bands of music with them and dance; to shake off the towns smoke, from their clothing, and other recreations. (Twamley, 1855)

Other modes of breaking the silence have been discovered in [horse-drawn] omnibuses oscillating between Birmingham and Sutton, with multitudes imported for a few hours respiration of Coldfield air. (Miss Bracken, 1860)

I happen to be between West Bromwich and Sutton Coldfield and every Monday during the Summer months there are half a dozen enormous Vans and Omnibuses full of excursionists passing our way . . . and besides there is the whole neighbourhood of Walsall who have no outlet – they would be only too glad to get to Sutton Park. (Sir Francis Scott, 1858)

The scheme of 1853 came to nothing, but when a railway line to Sutton finally opened in 1862 Sarah Holbeche noted on the first Sunday that over 2,000 people had visited the park: 'The sight at night when flocking to return such as never before had been or could have been supposed to be seen in this our hitherto quiet locality.'

The corporation needed to take action to control the activities of all these visitors, many of whom wanted to be entertained and provided with shelter, and had to be prevented from doing damage. Occasional resolutions such as 'Notice be given

Town Gate, c. 1890.

Advert in the 1890 Guide.   One of the attractions of the Crystal Palace.

warning parties coming to and returning from Sutton Park against their committing nuisances by waving flags and playing music on the Turnpike Road' were probably ineffective. More park-keepers were needed, and the money to pay for them was raised by introducing an entrance fee. On 19 August 1863 the warden and society resolved

> that in order to increase the number and efficiency of the force for maintaining order in the Park and protecting the inhabitants and respectable visitors from the lawless portion of the excursionists the Corporation consider it necessary to impose a payment per head upon all persons entering the Park not being inhabitants.

Extra security staff were taken on, and shelters and gates set up at Boldmere and Wyndley gates; Sutton residents were not charged, but other visitors had to pay 1d, or 3d on Thursdays, Fridays and Sundays. In 1870 there were over 72,000 such visitors, giving revenue of over £350, far more than the expense of the wages and other measures to protect the park.

Visitors could hire rowing boats at Wyndley Pool and Powells Pool, get refreshments at Hollyhurst Cottage, Blackroot Pool, Bracebridge Pool and Powells Pool, pay for pony and donkey rides, rest in any of the nine shelters provided or play on the swings and roundabouts. There were football and cricket pitches, a 'gallop' for horse-riders, and a golf course – originally nine holes near Town Gate in about 1880, then nine holes at Streetly in about 1890, increased to eighteen holes in 1894. Horse-racing in the park ended when the Four Oaks Park course was made in 1881; later the park was used for cross-country running and cyclo-cross races, and was a stage in the RAC Rally in the 1970s. The crowds flocking to the park were also catered for by the highly successful Royal Promenade Gardens, pleasure grounds laid out off Clifton Road near the Main Gate, outside the park. In 1879 a Crystal Palace was built in the gardens, capable of catering for over 2,000 people. Its attractions included a zoo, a miniature steam railway, and switchback rides. It thrived before the First World War and was still in business after the Second World War, but fell into disrepair and was demolished in the 1950s.

The park was the centrepiece for the jubilee celebrations of 1887 and 1897, and for the coronation festivities of 1902 and 1911. The corporation organised the local events on these royal occasions; for example, the coronation of King George V was celebrated with a programme of festivities on 22 and 23 June 1911. There were horse shows in two rings, at Meadow Plat and above Blackroot Pool, athletics on Meadow

Part of the avenue of lime trees planted in 1911.

Plat and swimming sports in Blackroot Pool. Brass bands played, there were firework displays in front of Park House, a dinner for old people at the Crystal Palace (the men were presented with a briar pipe and the women with half a pound of tea) and a children's tea for 2,772 schoolchildren in a tent on Meadow Plat. The children provided a large part of the entertainment, with a programme of maypole dances and tableaux from 3.00 p.m. to 7.00 p.m. on the first day, and a programme of school sports from 1.45 p.m. to 7.30 p.m. on the second. As well as their free tea, each child received one of the 3,200 commemorative medals which were struck, a coronation cup and a free ticket for a ride on either the switchback, the toy railway or one of the roundabouts in the Crystal Palace grounds. An avenue of trees was planted as a lasting tribute to the occasion.

The Annual Report of 1894 shows that the economic uses of the park were still important. Fifteen licences to sport (shoot game) were issued at £2 2s each; £68 6s 8d was received for depasturing 507 cows, 197 horses and 29 asses; gravel and sand was sold for £304. The saw mill at Blackroot (powered by a turbine) worked for 211 days and produced £569-worth of timber products. At that time Longmoor Mill and

Powell's Forge were still in operation, as well as the privately operated saw mill at Wyndley. There was no longer a mill at Park House, which had been converted into a handsome residence with extensive private grounds. The woods were being managed: over 50,000 young trees were planted, mostly larch and pine; 16 cartloads and 656 bundles of holly were provided at Christmas; fences were repaired around the woods as well as at the boundary; and the damage caused by a number of serious fires was recorded.

The park had frequently been used for military training, usually by part-time volunteer groups, using the old rifle range near Rowton's Hill and camping near Westwood Coppice. During the First World War military use of the park intensified: between 1914 and 1920 over 50,000 troops passed through the various camps, which were later used for convalescent officers and men, and finally by the New Zealand troops before they returned home. This is recorded on a tablet displayed near the main gate, but it does not record the military uses of the park in the Second World War, when various auxiliary forces were based there as well as prisoners of war. Part of the park was used for tank training, and tracts of land were brought into cultivation to meet the critical need for agricultural products. In 1957 an even greater number came to camp in Sutton Park for a while, but this was a peaceful occasion – the International Scout Jamboree.

The corporation often recorded a profit from its management of the park; every year from 1891 to 1905 receipts exceeded expenditure, the lion's share of the receipts being entrance fees paid at the gates. Charges for admission were

Part of the coronation celebrations in 1911.

Tree Planting.

An Avenue of Lime Trees will be planted leading from the Town Gate towards Blackroot. This will take place at 2-30 in the afternoon of Friday the 23rd June.

The Trees will be planted in the order set out below :—

No. 1	Mr. Councillor Cartwright (Mayor)	No	14	Mrs. Norris
„ 2	Mrs. Cartwright (Mayoress)	„	15	Mrs. Parkes
„ 3	Mrs. Glover	„	16	Mrs. Cooper
„ 4	Mrs. Walters	„	17	Mrs. Clarke
„ 5	Mrs. Emery	„	18	Mrs. Green
„ 6	Mrs. Seal	„	19	Mrs. Willmott
„ 7	Mrs. Vale	„	20	Mrs. Hooper
„ 8	Mrs. Sadler	„	21	Mrs. Pearson
„ 9	Mrs. Bailey	„	22	Mrs. Taylor
„ 10	Mrs. Walker	„	23	Mrs. Wareing
„ 11	Mrs. Millward	„	24	Mrs. Rathbone
„ 12	Miss Rabnett	„	25	Mrs. Parsons
„ 13	Mrs. Appleby	„	26	Mrs. Reay-Nadin
		„	27	Mrs. Clarry
		„	28	Mrs. T. Ellison

The Mayoress will present to each Lady a Silver Spade as a Souvenir (suitably inscribed).

Publicity poster,
c. 1890.

increased in 1908, and most years up to 1920 continued to show a profit. Many people came on horseback, 1,137 paying the fee in 1886, rising to 4,108 in 1902; 394 cyclists paid to go in in 1886, but the cycling boom was yet to come – there were 45,981 visitors in 1907. The first motor cars are recorded in 1903, when 62 were admitted, rising to 5,009 in 1924, no doubt keeping the forester and the twenty park-keepers on their toes. Sarah Holbeche may have thought the park was busy in 1862 when over 2,000

Publicity poster,
c. 1930.

A
HANDS-OFF THE PARK
MEETING

WILL BE HELD AT

Sutton Town Hall,

ON

SATURDAY, JANUARY 3rd,

AT EIGHT O'CLOCK, TO

Protest Against the Corporation Bill.

THE TOWN COUNCIL seek powers, amongst other things, which may enable them, if they desire to do so, **to construct Roads** and **run Motor 'Busses** through the Park.

To Build Cafés, Concert Halls, Refreshment Rooms, and " other buildings," **IN THE PARK,** and to **LET** them on **LEASE** for **TRADING PURPOSES.**

To ENCLOSE PARTS of the **PARK** for **Concerts, Cattle** and **Agricultural Shows** and other entertainments, and to **CHARGE for ADMISSION.**

To LAY OUT Golf Courses, **Cricket, Tennis** and **Bowling Greens,** and to **FENCE THEM IN,** and to **LET THEM TO PRIVATE CLUBS.**

To Devote the Income from the **Park** to the **Relief of the Rates.**

To MAKE BYE-LAWS as they choose in **DEFIANCE** of our **RIGHTS** and **PRIVILEGES** enjoyed by the inhabitants for over **300 Years**—in other words to

COMMERCIALIZE THE PARK.

Dr. A. H. EVANS, Chairman.

☞ No APATHY this Time!!

A Sutton Park idyll.

visitors came, but on Whit Monday 1933 a total of 51,902 people paid to go in, over 10,000 more than the previous record; on August Bank Holiday 1935 there were 45,234. Cattle were still being let into the park, about 250 head on average, but this number fell in the 1960s. After the severe drought of 1976 no more cattle were to be allowed in, but this soon resulted in the growth of young trees on the heathland and open pastures, and cattle were reintroduced as a conservation measure. Patterns of use began to change in the second half of the twentieth century, and by 1980 many of the facilities – boating on the pools, refreshment booths, water fountains, shelters and public lavatories – had gone, as the preservation of the park as a place of natural beauty, with unique habitats and an ancient landscape, came to be more appreciated. In 1997 it was designated a National Nature Reserve.

The survival of the park into the twenty-first century is the result of centuries of vigilance on the part of Suttonians. Bishop Vesey, by securing the charter of 1528 and providing the necessary livestock and fencing, gave the warden and society responsibility for a thriving park. When the warden and society sold off parts of the park as farmland, the inhabitants appealed to the courts and secured an injunction to prevent any further sales. When the first enclosure proposals were put forward in 1778 (including the park) they were defeated by popular demand. The Crystal Palace scheme of 1853 was defeated because the corporation would not give up part of the park to another body, and the agitation of 1855 died down when it appeared that reform might lead to the conversion of the park into market gardens. The corporation was vilified for not opposing the building of a railway line through the park in 1873, and in 1920 the Borough Council was forced to withdraw some clauses in its bill by a 'hands off the park' campaign. When the new Birmingham authority became responsible for the park in 1974 there was a policy of not maintaining park fences, but this was reversed by the strength of popular feeling. Fears that the park would be developed were dispelled by the special status given to it in the Unitary Development Plan of 1991. The continued influence of the Sutton Park Advisory Committee of Birmingham City Council, and the support given by local people through the Friends of Sutton Park Association, should ensure that the popular demand for the survival of Sutton Park will be strongly expressed in the future.

FOURTEEN

Sutton Coldfield – Just Another Suburb?

O n 31 March 1974 the Borough of Sutton Coldfield ceased to exist. The Local Government Act which came into force on 1 April that year merged Sutton and Birmingham into a new authority. Whereas before a council of forty people represented the ten wards of the borough and the mayor spent his year of office devoted to Sutton affairs, now the three new wards elected nine councillors to the new authority, and the lord mayor's visits to the town were few and far between. No doubt there were advantages in the new arrangements, and the City Council was right to treat the Sutton wards no differently from any other part of the new Birmingham, but how would Sutton survive without the forum of even a parish council to give it a focus?

By the end of 1974 all the large projects set in train in the last years of the old

The robe worn by successive mayors of Sutton Coldfield until 1974 is now on show in a display case in Sutton Coldfield Library – will it ever be worn again?

Shops on The Parade, c. 1970, (*Painting by George Gilbert*)

The Gracechurch Centre, which replaced the old Parade shops.

Sutton Coldfield Library was built as part of the Sainsbury Centre on the site of the old Empress Cinema.

Painting by George Gilbert of John Frost the Chemist's, c. 1970, then in its hey-day with specialist hi-fi, records and leather goods departments which have since closed.

council were complete – the swimming baths, the sport and leisure centre and youth centre near the former Crystal Palace, the Sainsbury Centre with its supermarket, multi-storey car park and state-of-the-art public library on the site of the former Empress Cinema, and the Gracechurch Centre where the Parade shops had been. These new facilities were on a scale suitable to a town the size of Sutton, and were greater than anything the major suburban centres of Birmingham could boast. Although they replaced buildings and facilities which were in decline or worn out, they lacked the character of the previous buildings, being imposed on their site rather than being formed by it. The new shopping centres thrived, but old specialist family firms like Gill's the toy shop and Hicks the outfitters closed down, and Frost the Chemist's struggled to survive. Both the architecture and the proliferation of chain stores gave an impression of anonymity, and many people thought that the demolition of the Parade shops was the end of Sutton.

The steady growth of new housing developments over former agricultural land continued, mostly in the form of large estates built by a single developer, adding to the impression of an anonymous suburb. New roads were named without reference to the features they replaced, and even in the surviving countryside hedges were being removed to convert the attractive patchwork of small fields into desolate prairie. There were other forces, however, working to counteract this drift towards a characterless commuter suburb. Buildings of architectural or historical value were protected by being added to the English Heritage lists, and conservation areas were

Manor Hill apartment blocks seen from the parish church car park, looking over the Gracechurch Centre and the bus terminus in Lower Parade.

designated (including High Street and Anchorage Road, the Four Oaks Park Estate and the Tudor Road complex) to which special planning rules applied.

The City Council has naturally been concentrating on regeneration in the centre of Birmingham and on improving the areas of deprivation elsewhere in the city, merely providing the requisite services to Sutton. Consequently, the development of the town has in part at least been the result of decisions made by the owners of property, rather than central planning by the local authority, and new projects have reinforced existing patterns. The site at Reddicroft was developed as offices, being near the High Street business quarter; at Newhall Street, opposite the Gracechurch Centre, a new shopping complex was built; and the old Manor Hill car park was developed as town centre apartment blocks. At the time of writing, there are planning applications pending for more apartments opposite Manor Hill, for more shops in Brassington Avenue, and for workshops and light manufacturing to the east of the town centre. Sutton seems likely to thrive as a business and commercial centre in the future, as success breeds success.

The final years of the Borough Council saw two important engineering works: the drainage scheme which put the E brook into an artificial channel and solved the problem of recurring floods, and the construction of the Sutton Coldfield bypass. A busy trunk road, the A38, used to run through the centre of Sutton, along The Parade, Mill Street and High Street, causing congestion and inconvenience; the bypass would relieve the pressure of through traffic, while another scheme, for a new road from Maney to the north end of Anchorage Road, would remove the commuter traffic. This latter road was the subject of many objections, and was never actually built, but it gave rise to discussions and pressure groups concerned with the civic life of Sutton. These issues of what is best for the town continue to be raised as major planning schemes are put forward, but so far without much success for the objectors. Even the green belt to the north and east of Sutton appears to be at the mercy of changes of use, with a golf course and a cemetery already agreed by the local authority. Central government has also approved the M6 toll motorway through the green belt, a large industrial site at Peddimore and a Premium Industrial Site at Ashfurlong. These last two developments may well change the character of Sutton in the twenty-first century.

New housing in Sutton has generally reflected the existing mix, predominantly semi-detached and small detached houses with some more luxurious developments and a growing number of apartments and sheltered housing schemes. The general perception of Sutton as a desirable place to live has been retained; the address has a certain cachet, reflected in the price of houses. As a commuter town, it has benefited from recent trends; there are many more restaurants and bars in the town centre, as eating out has become more common; health clubs and sports facilities are abundant; and the banning of traffic from the town centre has been a great improvement. Equally, the town suffers from the modern problems of graffiti, litter and vandalism; there are eyesores in neglected corners; while crime and the fear of crime result in the frequent shattering of the peace by strident burglar alarms and the wailing sirens of emergency vehicles.

New housing estates sometimes included services such as shops, schools, community centres and churches, for example the council estate at Falcon Lodge (*c.* 1950), the mixed council/private estate at Hill West (*c.* 1963), and the private estates at New Oscott (*c.* 1965) and Walmley Ash (*c.* 1980). Many of the other estates relied on existing services (Ley Hill, *c.* 1960; Somerville, *c.* 1962; Heath Croft, *c.* 1965; Hill Hook, *c.* 1978; Froggatts Farm, *c.* 1985; Walmley Road, *c.* 2000; Duttons Lane, *c.* 2002, among others). The existing suburban centres at Boldmere and Walmley grew busier, but were overshadowed by the vast supermarket developments at Walmley Ash and on the site of the former Princess Alice Children's Home at the Beggar's Bush, while the other two major centres, at Mere Green and Wylde Green, were able to expand and accommodate new supermarkets and facilities, with further growth planned. These centres reinforce the concept of Sutton as a growing town with its own suburbs.

A large number of clubs and societies flourish in the town, including two little theatres, other dramatic societies, a chamber orchestra and light opera groups. The Town Hall is an important venue for many of these, and when in 1997 the city

Green Belt near Peddimore, where the requirements of modern agriculture have reduced a pleasant landscape of fields and hedges to a dull prairie.

Green Belt at Fox Hill Road, the proposed Premium Industrial Site.

Green Belt near Langley Mill, the M6 toll road under construction.

declared it could no longer afford to keep it in good repair, a users' group was set up which was able to raise money in the form of grants so that a thorough restoration of the building could be carried out. The previous year another Sutton building, New Hall Mill, which had been restored in 1970 by the owner, began a series of open days thanks to another voluntary group, the Friends of New Hall Mill. All manner of sport is catered for in the town by various sports clubs, including an athletics track at Wyndley, and there are seven golf courses.

Just to the east of Sutton is the Belfry Golf Centre, a venue for international matches. A major event at the Belfry fills Sutton's hotels, which had grown considerably in size and number in the last years of the twentieth century. Enough visitors are attracted to the town to sustain thirteen hotels, some of them very large, but there is no official organisation promoting the attractions of Sutton, no

Bronze statue by Benjamin Cresswell, 1920. It is of a man teaching a young boy to swim, part of a war memorial for Boldmere Swimming Club.

Mural in sand-blasted concrete at Sutton Coldfield Library, depicting scenes from the town's history.

The totem pole sculpture in Sutton Park.

guidebook and no visitors' centre, except for Sutton Park. Here the attraction has been recognised, not only in its designation as a national nature reserve and in its scheduling as an ancient monument, but also in the provision of a Park Visitors' Centre with its own guidebook. As in the 1970s, when the Cresswell sculpture was installed at the new swimming baths and a mural was commissioned for the new library (its unveiling was the last official act of the Borough Council, on 31 March 1974), so in 1997 a work of art marked the new nature reserve status of Sutton Park. Carved from solid oak by the sculptor Graham Jones, the 3.5-metre totem pole depicts the wild life in the park. It appears to spring from a giant acorn, symbolising renewal and new life, and helping to give all those who live in Sutton a sense of place in the new millennium.

Bibliography

(The unpublished items are all in Sutton Coldfield Reference Library)

Source Materials

Sutton Coldfield Library has a good collection of original and copied source materials, including Corporation Records from 1886 to 1974.

Fentiman, A.F., A *Sutton Coldfield Source Book in three parts*, unpublished, 1989. (An annotated list of Sutton Coldfield documents in the Record Offices of the Midlands)

Beresford, M., *Sutton Coldfield: a calendar of the documentary references 1066–1528*, unpublished, c. 1939. (Mostly Public Record Office references)

Calendar of Old Documents of the Corporation of Sutton Coldfield to 1860, unpublished, n.d. (The official Borough Records, now housed in Birmingham Reference Library)

Histories of Sutton Coldfield

Bedford, W.K. Riland, *History of Sutton Coldfield*, Birmingham, 1891.

Bracken, A.A., *The Forest and Chase of Sutton Coldfield*, London, 1860.

Dugdale, W., *The Antiquities of Warwickshire*, 1656, but the 1730 edition is usually used, also reprinted, Manchester, Morten, 1973.

History of Sutton Coldfield by an Impartial Hand, unpublished, 1762.

Jones, D.V., *The Royal Town of Sutton Coldfield*, Westwood Press, 1979.

Lea, R.M., *Scenes from Sutton's Past*, Westwood Press, 1989.

Midgley, W., *A Short History of Sutton Coldfield Town and Chase*, Birmingham, 1904.

Moss, H., *A Royal Town and its Park*, Sutton Coldfield, 1977.

Proceedings of the Sutton Coldfield Local History Research Group (SCLHRG), Vols 1–6, SCLHRG, 1992– 2002

Twamley, Z., *History of Sutton Coldfield*, unpublished, 1855.

Victoria History of the County of Warwick, vol. IV, Oxford University Press, 1947.

Pictorial Histories

Bates, S., *Sutton Coldfield: a Pictorial History*, Phillimore, 1997.

Baxter, M., *The Old Photographs Series: Sutton Coldfield*, Chalford, 1994.

Baxter, M., *Sutton Coldfield, Second Selection*, Chalford, 1997.

Baxter, M. and Field, *Then and Now: Sutton Coldfield*, Tempus, 2002.

Special Subjects

Bedford, W.K. Riland, *Three hundred years of a Family Living*, Birmingham, 1889. (Rectors of Sutton Coldfield)

Cobbold, P., A *Study of Local Government in Sutton Coldfield in the later eighteenth and nineteenth centuries*, unpublished, 1971.

Evans, N.G., *Investigation of Holy Trinity Church, Sutton Coldfield*, unpublished, 1988.

Field, D.J., *The History of Sutton Coldfield Municipal Charities*, Brewin Books, 2011.

Hodder, M., 'Continuity and Discontinuity in the Landscape; Roman to Medieval in Sutton Chase' *Medieval Archaeology* vol. 36, 1992 (Prehistory)

Holbeche Diaries. Recollections of Sutton in the Nineteenth century by Richard, Helen and Sarah Holbeche, J. Jordan (ed), unpublished.

Horsfall, J., *The Ironmasters of Penns*, Roundwood, 1971. (Penns Mill)

Lea, R.M., *The Quarters of Sutton*, SCLHRG, 1981. (Hearth Tax returns)

Lea, R.M., *Steaming up to Sutton*, Westwood, 1984. (First railway line)

Osbourne, K., *A History of Bishop Vesey's Grammar School*, Sutton Coldfield, 1990.

Sidwell, G. and Durant, W.J., *The Popular Guide to Sutton and Park*, Birmingham, 1890, 1893, 1900.

Background

Dyer, C., *Hanbury*, Leicester University Press, 1991. (Prehistory)

Sawyer, P., *Domesday Book: a reassessment*, Arnold, 1987. (Domesday)

Carpenter, C., *Locality and Polity, a study of Warwickshire Landed Society, 1401–1499*, Cambridge University Press, 1992. (Late medieval)

Heal, F., *Of Prelates and Princes*, Cambridge University Press, 1980. (Bishops under Henry VIII)

Hughes, A., *Politics, Society and Civil War in Warwickshire 1620–1660*, Cambridge University Press, 1987. (Civil War)

Wrigley, E.A. and Schofield, R.S., *Population History of England 1541–1871*, Arnold, 1980. (Population)

Neeson, J., *Commoners*, Cambridge University Press, 1993. (Enclosure of the Commons)

Additional Sources

Chapter 1

Wills, L.J., *The Triassic Succession in the Central Midlands*, in the Quarterly Journal of the Geological Society, 1970.

Warrington, G., *et al. A Correlation of Triassic rocks in the British Isles*, Geological Society of London Special Report 13, 1980.

Gilbert, C.J., *The Geology of Sutton Coldfield: a paper read before the Vesey Club*, 1890.

Horsfall, J., *The Ironmasters of Penns*, Roundwood, 1971.

Rackham, O., *Trees and Woodland in the British Landscape*, Dent, 1976.

Birmingham and Warwickshire Archaeological Society Field Group East of Sutton Survey. *Interim Reports*, 1995–9.

Hodder, M., 'Continuity and Discontinuity in the landscape; Roman to Medieval in Sutton Chase', *Medieval Archaeology*, vol. 36, 1992.

Dyer, C., *Lords and peasants in a changing society*, Cambridge, 1980.

Hooke, D and S. Burnell, *Landscape and Settlement in Britain*, Exeter University Press, 1995.

Dodgshon, R.A. & Butlin, R.A., *A Historical Geography of England and Wales*, Academic Press, p. 1978.

Chapter 2

Walmsley, J.F.R., 'The censarii of Burton Abbey and the Domesday population'. *North Staffordshire Journal of Field Studies*, vol. VII, 1968.

Hodder, M., *The Early Development of the Coldfield. Transactions of the South Staffordshire Archaeological and Historical Society for 1990–1.*

Rackham, O., *Trees and Woodland in the British Landscape*, Dent, 1976.

Victoria History of the County of Stafford, vol. 3, Oxford University Press, 1970.

Darby, H.C. and Campbell, *The Domesday Geography of South-East England*, Cambridge University Press, 1962.

Birrell, J., *Hunting and the Royal Forest.* Published in the Papers of the Conference *L'uomo e la Foresta*, Prato, Italy, 1996.

Chapter 3

Birmingham Reference Library deed 348038.

The Beauchamp Cartulary, Pipe Roll Society, vol. 81, 1980.

Birmingham University Field Archaeology Unit. *An Archaeological evaluation at Peddimore*, 1998.

Personal communication from Dr Mike Hodder.

Chapter 4

New Shipton 2000, a photographic survey of New Shipton, Sutton Reference Library.

Charters in the Bridgeman papers at Stafford County Record Office.

Birmingham Reference Library Archives, Digby A, 258, 260.

MLM 134/3 in the Middleton Papers, Nottingham University Library, transcribed and annotated in volume 6 of the *Proceedings of the Sutton Coldfield Local History Research Group*, 2001.

Chapter 4

Ross, C., *The Estates and Finances of Richard Beauchamp*, Earl of Warwick, Dudgdale Society Occasional Paper no. 12, 1956.

The bailiff's compotus (Stratford Record Office BRT 1/3/180) is translated and annotated in volume 5 of the *Proceedings of the Sutton Coldfield Local History Research Group*, 1999.

Chapter 5

Leland, *Itinerary*, c. 1546, trans. Lucy Toulmin Smith, London, Bell 1906.

Lease of the Town Mill to Thomas Keene, 1533; deed in Sutton Library.

Dictionary of National Biography.

Guy, J.A., *The Cardinal's Court*, Harvester, 1977.

Guy, J.A., *The Public Career of Sir Thomas More*, Harvester, 1980.

Charters of Sutton Coldfield, a translation published by Sutton Coldfield Corporation in 1935.

Birmingham Reference Library Deed 206601.

Chapter 6

The Sutton Coldfield Parish Register is in the Warwickshire County Record Office; it has been transcribed and indexed by the Sutton Coldfield Local History Research Group, and a copy of this transcription is in Sutton Reference Library.

Laslett, P., *The World we have lost*, Methuen, 1993.

Transcribed and indexed in Lea, R.M., *The Quarters of Sutton*, 1981

There are photocopies of the seventeenth century probate records for Sutton Coldfield, transcribed and indexed, in Sutton Reference Library.

Eddowes Perry and Osbourne no.141, in Sutton Reference Library.

Lea, R.M. and Booth, *New Hall Mill: history and machinery*, Sutton Coldfield, 1999.

Minutes of the Warden and Society.

The 'Compton Census'; the Warwickshire section is printed in Ratcliff, S.C. and Johnson,
    Warwickshire County Records, vol. VII, 1946.
Warwickshire County Records, vol. VIII, 1953.
Borsay, P., 'Early Modern Urban Landscapes, 1540–1800', in *The English Urban Landscape*, Philip
    Waller, 2000.
Sutton Borough Record no. 80, Birmingham Reference Library.
Holbeche Diary.
Sutton Borough Records no. 78/216-260, Birmingham Reference Library.
Lillywhite, J., *The Corn Rent map and survey of Sutton Colfield*, unpublished, typescript in Sutton
    Reference Library.

Chapter 8
Report on the proceedings of an Inquiry . . . held in August 1855.
Minutes of the Warden and Society of Sutton Coldfield.

Chapter 9
Quarter Sessions Rolls, Shrewsbury Borough Records.
Bate, W. Jackson, *Samuel Johnson*, Chatto and Windus, 1978. Nicholas Ford was warden of Sutton
    Coldfield in 1709.
Minutes of the Warden and Society.

Chapter 10
Riland Bedford, W.K., *Three hundred years of a Family Living*, London, 1889.
Osbourne, K., *A History of Bishop Vesey's Grammar School*, Sutton Coldfield ,1990.
Quoted in the *Souvenir Programme of Coronation Festivities*, 1911

Chapter 11
Advert in *The Miller*, a trade journal.
Transcript of a tape-recording of a talk by the late James Speight to the Sutton Rotary Club, c. 1968.
Recollections of the late William Bubb, recorded in 1984.

Chapter 12
Warden and Society Committee Minutes.
Eliot, G., *Adam Bede*, 1859.
Thompson, F., *Lark Rise to Candleford*, 1945.
Eddowes Perry and Osbourne document 108, Sutton Reference Library, 1994.

Chapter 13
Riland Bedford, W.K., 'Our Native Sculptor', in *The Warden*, vol. 3, 1898.
Horton, H.H., *Sutton Park: a poem*, 1850. The superior verses by Charles Barker, headmaster of
    the Grammar School, *A Guide to the Sutton Park Bazaar*, are printed in vol. 1 of *The Warden*,
    1898.

Chapter 14
City of Birmingham, *Birmingham Unitary Development Plan*, 1989
The Birmingham Plan, 1993
The Birmingham Plan: alterations

Index